August 25, 1994

To Jean —

You couldn't do anything?!
You are terrific — on the
committee and as a friend —

Love,

Marlys

All I Could Do Was Love You

ALL
I COULD DO
WAS
LOVE YOU

The True Story
of a Daughter's Courage
and a Mother's Devotion

Marlys Lehmann

ADLER&ADLER

Published in the United States in 1988 by
Adler & Adler, Publishers, Inc.
4550 Montgomery Avenue
Bethesda, Maryland 20814

Library of Congress Cataloging-in-Publication Data

Lehmann, Marlys, 1933–
    All I could do was love you.

    1. Lehmann, Alison—Health.   2. Amputation of leg—
Patients—United States—Biography.   3. Lehmann,
Marlys, 1933–   . Family.   4. Mothers—United States—
Biography.   I. Title.
RD560.L44L44   1988   362.4'3'0924 [B] 87–25479
ISBN 0–917561–48–1

Printed in the United States of America
First Edition

Grateful acknowledgment is made to Warner Bros. Music
for permission to reprint selections from "Broken Wings"
by Richard Page, Steve George, and John Lang.
Copyright © 1985 Warner-Tamerlane Publishing Corp.
& Entente Music. All rights reserved. Used by permission.

To Alison
All I could do was love you

Contents

One

THE BEGINNING, THE END

On July 25, 1985, Alison was sixteen years old and in the midst of the happiest summer of her life. At 2:45 in the afternoon she had two legs. At midnight, she had one.

In the instant that a ton of blue steel pinned her leg against a telephone pole, shattering it, Alison's care-free life was finished.

Alison knew nothing of my being called to the receptionist's office of the company where I work. I knew nothing as I hurried to the police car waiting outside. A big policeman with a thick black mustache, a courier sent by Englewood Hospital, said, "Get in. Your daughter is in the hospital. I'll take you there." The officer, all business, looked straight ahead as he engaged the gears.

"What happened?" I asked, while the inane question, Will I remember what date this is? slipped through my mind. I thought of Alison swimming at a county park with her friend Heather. "She was at Darlington today. Did she get hurt swimming?" My voice was calm. Alison is an excellent swimmer.

"Car accident."

Car. Oh, my God. Heather was new to the wheel. I envisioned truck-laden Route 17. "A car crash!"

"She was a pedestrian."

"Where was she? Where was she hit? Is she alive?" But he knew, or was saying, no more. He pushed a button and the whirl of the red light on the roof reflected on the car's white hood. The siren blared, disturbing the quiet of a summer afternoon in a small suburban city.

The officer remained silent. Though I sensed his empathy, he said no more until he pulled up to the hospital's ambulance entrance.

Alison is in here, I thought, but they're not taking me to her. A social worker met us and ushered me into a small room, away from the open waiting room where I had at times waited for my little boys' arms to be set or their cuts to be stitched. Warren Earabino, Alison's summertime employer and father of her friend Jenni, met me at the emergency room and put his arms around me. Why is Warren here? Alison wasn't at work today; he wouldn't know what happened to her.

Warren spoke quietly. "Alison was with Jenni today, Marlys. They went to a sidewalk sale and were walking home on Piermont Road. A car went out of control, off the street, and into the girls. Jenni was thrown, but Alison was pinned to a telephone pole. It's her leg, and she has other injuries. She's badly hurt." With that, he slipped away to return to Jenni, also injured.

Something like this can't be happening again, I thought, not to somebody who has already lost a child. But the two doctors who sat down opposite me said, "She's going to lose her leg."

It's not a dream, it's not a nightmare. I knew that from having lived through another such moment, a moment when another doctor said, "It's leukemia." Those words in 1964 were the portent of death for Andrew, who was then seven. These words were the portent of a life changed forever for Alison, my lovely girl.

Just as in 1964, this was a July day. It was as difficult to fathom now, "She's going to lose her leg," as it was then, "It's leukemia."

Why?

Why my child?

But, far back, over almost twenty years of lonely memory, I remembered answering that silent question, Why not my child?

The doctors wanted to operate immediately, fearing for Alison's life. "But we can't just take her leg without another opinion, without trying everything to save it. Can we move her to a New York hospital, where they have had more experience in accidents such as this?" I asked. When the doctor called my husband, Charly responded to the idea of immediate surgery to remove Alison's leg just as I had. We had to try every means to avoid such a final step. Englewood Hospital would stabilize her; she would then be moved to Bellevue Hospital, to the care of a microsurgical team that had a world-renowned record of reattaching limbs.

3

Finally, they let me see Alison. She lay on a stretcher in a room by herself, covered to the chest by a sheet. They had removed her clothes, cut them off, probably. I tried not to imagine the scene of the accident, the frantic hands trying to save her. If I had difficulty believing what had happened, the moments I spent with Alison convinced and horrified me. She was conscious—so conscious. White under her summer tan, she looked lost in her terror.

But she wasn't in pain. The shock was too great to allow pain to penetrate. Through dry lips she whispered, "What happened?" When I told her she had been struck by a car, she asked where she had been and with whom. I wanted to gather her into my arms, to comfort her, comfort myself, but the life-sustaining tubes attached to her and my fear of hurting her further allowed me only to stroke the mass of dirtied and tangled dark hair away from her cold forehead.

"I love you, Alison, I love you." It was all I could say.

Two

BELLEVUE

Friday, July 26, 2:15 A.M.

Somehow, I must make this real. I must write down my thoughts as I sit here in a room that Bellevue has lent to Charly and me so that we may mourn privately. Twenty years ago, I kept a journal through Andrew's illness, at first as a catharsis, then, as time passed, to testify to his courage. I wanted others to know him as I had, but on the day he died I put the notebook away and have been unable to look at it since. Now I feel I must write again, to try to think through the unthinkable. Maybe my writing will certify the enormity of what is happening. It has been a long day, a long night. Our lives have been transformed, not in a long day or a long night, but in an instant, an instant when metal hit flesh.

The fifteen-mile ambulance trip from Englewood, New Jersey, across the George Washington Bridge, over the Hudson River to New York, and down Manhattan's Harlem River and East River drives can be negotiated in a half-hour if there is no traffic. But in New York and New Jersey's evening rush hour the trip often takes an hour or longer. It didn't take us that long. An Englewood police car led the ambulance from the hospital grounds and through the busy evening streets of Englewood to the Bridge Plaza, where a Port Authority police car was positioned to take over as escort. Across the bridge, a New York City squad car picked up the task, shepherding the ambulance the rest of the way to Bellevue Hospital. Despite my anguish, I marveled at the precise timing and the attention being given to one little girl in terrible trouble.

Without its escort on the car-choked highway, the ambulance might have been ignored by New York's homebound drivers. But the police car had a more than piercing siren and threatening red lights. It was driven by a policeman who bellowed intermittently into a bullhorn, "Outta the way," in a tone they understood. Like the Red Sea, a lane opened grudgingly for the ambulance, and the trip took only long minutes. The squad car, ambulance on its tail, exited directly into Bellevue's emergency area on Thirtieth Street.

God, please.

It was all I could think. But what was the prayer? That Alison's leg would be saved? That she could continue her previously blessed life? That her beauty would remain unblemished? It was unfathomable that Alison would lose her leg, but I couldn't pray for what could not be, and I feared that keeping her leg was not to be. It had happened then, too, twenty years ago. Once the diagnosis of leukemia—certain death—had been made, I couldn't pray that Andrew's life would be saved. That would be putting God into a corner. I prayed then for strength for Andrew and for a peaceful and dignified death, and that prayer was answered. But I hadn't reached a point in the ambulance where I could pray for strength for Alison, and I can't even now, alone, at midnight in this room that is not my own.

It has been about seven hours since we got here, Alison and I, about two hours since they removed her leg. I saw only that her eyes were closed when the ambulance arrived, and then the stretcher vanished through tall double doors. There was no one near me anymore, except the New York City police officer, who sat with me in the little anteroom where I had been directed to wait. I was on one of four chairs on one side of the garishly lit space, he on one of the straight-backed chairs opposite me. He didn't speak. I was grateful.

Bellevue's emergency room was calmer than I would have expected of such a huge hospital. There were stretchers standing helter skelter inside the outer doorway. One person lay far down on a cot, curled in the fetal position, dirty bare feet extended over the edge. Another, an old woman, lay face up, calling for attention. Neither seemed gravely ill or wounded.

I wanted Charly with me, but I knew it would take him nearly two hours to get to Bellevue from his office, which involved a tunnel crossing and a trip through crawling city traffic. The policeman, arms resting between open knees, looked down at the floor. He would not leave until my husband came, said this representative of New York's finest.

Nearly an hour passed before a red-bearded man introduced himself as Dr. Livingston. He sat, leaving an empty seat between us. He didn't look at me. "We can't save her leg," he said.

His voice was low but authoritative, not to be argued with. But I argued. "Try again. Check some more," I implored. "Can't the microsurgical team do anything? They saved the legs of a woman pinned under a crane for hours. That had to be worse. Please, please try again." Numbness vanished; steely control vanished.

He agreed to return to Alison, to continue trying. First, however, he used a word I hadn't heard yet that day. Her leg had been "severed," held together after the accident only by a thin strand, a tendon, skin—I didn't know what. I didn't hear, I didn't want to hear. What was left below that was shattered; the ligaments, the muscles, the nerves.

It was moments after Charly arrived and the policeman left that Dr. Livingston, followed by his surgical team of half a dozen young men, again sat beside me. Gently, they explained to us why it was necessary to— impossible not to—remove Alison's leg. We had to accept it. Each one spoke; each added another detail to seal the case. It was the anguished face of one of the doctors that convinced me they had done all they could do. "We are here to save limbs, not to amputate them," this doctor said, so softly I could barely hear him.

They let us in to see Alison for a moment before she was taken away to surgery. Beyond the double doors she lay. "Do they have to amputate my leg?" she whispered as I laid my head down on the stretcher near hers. Though I wasn't sure she understood what

8

it all meant, I was glad that someone else had said the word "amputate" to her. One of my fears was her reaction, upon awakening, to the discovery of a missing leg.

Four hours later, after midnight, Dr. Livingston told us the amputation was completed. Though her leg had been severed below the knee, he couldn't save her knee. It was shattered beyond repair. We didn't understand what meaning those words had until Dr. Livingston demonstrated the limp she will always have. Above the knee means a difficult rehabilitation. It means disability. Disabled. The word is new to me.

Below the knee would have meant a far easier time for Alison. I understand.

Just as we became experts in leukemia, the disease and its treatment, between July 8, 1964, and April 13, 1966, the years of Andrew's illness, we are now about to become experts on amputation. I felt Dr. Livingston's regret at the loss of Alison's knee. Surely, I thought, this chief resident in trauma surgery must remove legs and knees every day. One more can't make much difference, but it seemed to.

Now I'm alone. A Bellevue social worker took us into a private room after we tore ourselves from Alison. Someone has furnished this room to give solace, with two blue fabric-covered reclining chairs, a small sofa, a round table and four chairs, and two hassocks. A bank of windows, shuttered now to keep out the lights of the parking area outside, is on one side of the room.

The couple who lives next door to us were among the first to hear of the accident. They sped to Bellevue

Hospital to be with us and were there, ready to help us through the difficult hours since we left Alison in the emergency room. For almost four hours they sat with us, but finally, near midnight, I convinced them to leave. I needed time alone with Charly. As always, Charly and I required no words.

Now, Alison is still in surgery, with other doctors, orthopedists, inserting a rod into the broken femur of the amputated leg and checking further on her broken hip and pelvis. The concussion she sustained will heal by itself, the doctors tell us. After Dr. Livingston spoke to us, I begged Charly to go home too, to take care of our animals—three cats, two dogs—and to try to sleep. We've had a few hours alone together, enough to share our sorrow, enough to wonder what will become of our daughter's dreams.

Friday, July 26, 4:30 A.M.

The two orthopedists who came in a half hour ago said they have completed the operation, Alison is in the recovery room, and I can see her soon. I'm amazed that I may visit her in the recovery room. It's not all rules and regulations here. Bellevue, which probably has the highest rate of trauma emergencies in the city, possibly in the world, is treating us as individuals in the course of another busy day. I've seen it all night. When I tried to rest and found that I had a choice of either bright fluorescent overhead lights or utter darkness—the latter unthinkable—I found a janitor, who went out of his way to find a bulb for one of the floor lamps in the room. Later, he helped me adjust the window so that I could keep out the pelting rain that broke a months-long drought.

The rain adds to my loneliness; I should be at home in my own bed, hearing the welcome rain against the wall behind the headboard, knowing that my child is safe in her own room, her own bed, the floral-print sheets high up over her head as they always are, the shelves of furry animals covering half of one wall, and at least one cat or dog asleep at the foot of her bed.

Instead, I'm here, and my child is not safe. This, too, I've felt before, first in the high gray hospital beside a dying child, and days afterward, hearing rain on a cold April night, knowing it was falling as well on the newly filled grave of my nine-year-old child.

I can't close my eyes. But even with eyes open, I see nothing but Alison. I see her as she was two days ago, as she left my car and walked into the house. I watched her in her tiny—so tiny—royal-blue shorts. She is just over five feet tall, but her legs are—were—long for her height, straight and slim like the rest of her. She is— has been—an animated, happy teenager. Her eyes laugh when she is happy, and she is—was—happy most of the time. Since May, she has enjoyed her job as an attendant at the pool of Tammy Brook Country Club in town and has gained through it a new sense of accomplishment. She is at her best with her peers. With most adults she is quiet, rarely showing her exuberance. But this has been a summer of friendships and fun and dates, the happiest of her life; she told me so every day.

When Alison was very young, still in the feminine

little dresses I tried to keep on my only daughter as long as possible, one of her day-camp counselors called her tough. My little girl, I thought, my baby girl, tough? I discounted it. But as Alison got older, I realized that the counselor was right. Alison is afraid of nothing, except spiders.

But Alison is tender, too. She is kind, compassionate, and tolerant of others. She understands some people's need to behave differently or oddly. She is affectionate with animals, particularly cats. I see her as just emerged from childhood. Though unsophisticated in a world where many sixteen-year-olds have long since considered themselves adults, she is capable, intelligent, forthright, and independent. Or, she has been.

Alison was born two and a half years after Andrew died. In the Jewish tradition of using someone's first initials to memorialize that person, we named her Alison Diane for Andrew David. She looks like him, but she looks like her two other brothers, too. Jonathan, thirteen when Alison was born, was an intense child, still deeply hurt by the loss of his best friend, his alter ego, the brother who had been just ten and a half months younger than he. Peter was five and a half at Alison's birth. He was an imp who brought sunshine where there was gloom and trouble where there was calm. Peter fell in love with Alison from the start. He was mother, father, brother, sister—whatever she wanted of him—when they played "house." He built block houses and card houses and doll houses for her. Alison came into our lives when we were most vulnerable, when we most needed her.

Three

INTENSIVE CARE

Friday, July 26, 6:00 P.M.

Before dawn, ten hours after the operation began, I
saw Alison. Afterward, I telephoned Charly and cried,
and he came back to the hospital. Since then they have
let us into the recovery room every hour or so, just
long enough for us to touch her, to look at her, and
know that she is alive. She's been there all day, though
we are told now that she'll soon be moved to pediatric
intensive care. A tube is down her throat, helping her
to breathe. Others are attached to her, on her chest,
on her hand, seemingly everywhere, lifelines between
her and the droning monitors that tell the new story
of Alison. She doesn't react to us. Her eyes, when they
are open, are lifeless, staring without comprehension.
I am frightened, once again prisoner in a hospital,
dependent on others to keep my child alive.

I knew that I would see the outline of what was
once Alison's left leg. Beneath the sheet there is half
a leg. Her stump. She is disabled. I have to say it to
myself, because it is so and I have to help her know it
is so. Her life is changed. Is it over?

One of the people I thought of last night was our neighbor, Wayne Siegmann, now thirty-four. When he was fifteen, a teenager in Cresskill at just about the time when Andrew was dying, he was struck by one of the evening freight trains going through town. He lost his leg, high up above the knee. I knew about it, and at the time, though I was losing my own son, I couldn't imagine Wayne's mother's anguish. Did she imagine her son's foot and leg, cut off, separate from him? Wayne's injury was grotesque; how did it strike the woman who had borne him?

Now Wayne is married. He and his wife, Eileen, have four children. When Wayne and Eileen bought the house across the street from us, I knew what kind of person he was. I had watched him climb the high diving board of the town pool just months after his accident, climb it with one leg and a stump, and dive in. With that gesture, he demonstrated to all who saw him how he felt toward himself, how he wanted them to feel toward him. A few years ago Wayne built a second story on his house, with the help of his father-in-law and a friend. Wayne climbed the ladder. Wayne lugged the lumber. Alison has seen Wayne's accomplishments, has seen the second story go up, has heard of his dive into the pool. Wayne's life is not over.

All day friends have come to see us in the room Bellevue has allowed us to use until Alison comes out of the recovery room. I lived only for the moments when we could be with Alison, but to others, the friends who didn't know what to say or do, I tried to appear whole. Conversations droned past me, above me, through me. I wanted none of them.

A neighbor: "It's much better that it's her leg than her arm. Prosthetics for legs are so much better than they are for arms." Are they? I don't know anything about prosthetics.

A friend: "But you've *got* to attend next month's wedding. You're wrong to make this decision now." I can't even think of what I'll do in an hour. I can't think.

A doctor-friend: "Shall I prescribe a tranquilizer for you?" No, no. I must feel this, much as it hurts, just as I felt my way through Andrew's illness and death, so that I can come to accept it.

Our rabbi, Fred Pomerantz, with the first words that penetrated, that mattered: "Everyone in the temple is shocked, asking me what they can do for you. I've told them not to call you. But how can they help?"

"Rabbi, tell them to write to us, to write whatever they're thinking, whatever they want to tell us. It will help us and it will help them. I don't want to talk, don't want visitors, but I do want Alison to know how much others care."

A Bellevue psychiatrist assigned to our case and visiting us in the room: "She will have to face reality. She must remember all the events of the day, even the actual impact, so as to face reality. We will visit her every day and help her work her way through."

The idea that Alison will remember the accident is more than I can bear. I can't imagine it happening. I can't imagine how I will react to her pain and sorrow, this child who has had need for few tears in her sixteen years of life.

Charly, to the others in the room: "Thank God it's her left leg. She can still drive." Ah, the difference between a man and a woman, a father and a mother. I hadn't thought about which leg it was, just that it was a leg, gone.

And, Charly again: "We have to be grateful. We have to think that we might have been in a funeral home instead of here." Charly has said this many times. Yes, she was millimeters, microseconds, away from death. The broken bones on the one side and the telephone pole on the other shielded her internal organs from the destruction inflicted upon her.

Charly is certain Alison will be all right, will be strong, will live her life fully. Alison, in her teen years, has said her father doesn't understand her. I hope she is wrong.

Friday, July 26, 10:00 P.M.

Alison has been moved to intensive care, and I am permitted to stay, even sleep, beside her. She and I are left with the nurses and the other patients in the unit. Peter, who has come from Dartmouth, where he is spending the summer following his graduation, has seen Alison and has left for the night with Charly. I'm surprised that we are allowed to visit Alison in this room for very sick children and that I am permitted to spend the night. My bed is a blue plastic chair, its back at an unrelenting sixty-degree angle. I think, though, that I can sleep even here because it has been two days and a night since I last slept. I will pull up another chair and sleep across the two of them as best I can.

Just as I reacted to the size of the emergency room, I'm surprised that Bellevue's pediatric intensive-care room isn't larger. It contains Alison's, another bed, and two cribs with sleeping babies. In the other bed is another sixteen-year-old teenager, also struck by a car, but while he was riding a bicycle. He, six feet tall when he was able to stand, has spinal injuries. He is paralyzed from the neck down.

Now I can pray. Thank you, God. Thank you that we are not sitting in the funeral home Charly spoke of. Thank you, God, that Alison is not paralyzed. And please, God, give the boy's parents strength. Give us strength. Give Alison strength.

Alison is aware and awake, but her eyes are expressionless, as though if she were to allow herself to feel it would be unbearable. The respirator whooshes continually, helping her to breathe. Her heart is working so hard and so fast that I can count the beats at the side of her neck.

"Am I going to die?" she asks me.

"Alison, I promise you—it is all I can promise you—but I promise you, you are not going to die."

She remembers nothing of the accident. She remembers nothing of the whole day.

"What happened?" she asks again and again. When I tell her, she asks whom was she with, where was she, why was she with Jenni. It makes no more sense to her than it does to me.

There is little pain. The morphine doesn't allow pain, and she is still affected by the anesthesia. The nurses are kind and caring, just as Dr. Livingston said they would be. We are dependent on them, and I can't imagine anyone being more gracious than these women are.

Alison asks about the boy to her left who fills the bed from end to end and who doesn't move his head to look at her. She understands. "It's better to lose one limb than four," she whispers.

Saturday, July 27, 7:15 A.M.

My day revolves around the morphine shots, necessary now because Alison hurts everywhere: the stump, the broken pelvic area, the broken hip, her back, so much so that they have put her on a foam mattress with deep impressions, like an egg carton, to ease the pain. Moving her even the smallest amount is torture for her. After she receives morphine, I know she will sleep, and that is when I go into the hall to telephone. When I hear Charly's voice, I sob.

I cry with Alison, too. I want her to know it's all right for her to cry. But she doesn't, only stares with empty eyes. She wakes often during the night. She's aware each time a nurse comes near her, and I'm thankful this happens frequently, for monitoring is constant in the ICU.

Once, she awoke and asked, "Did they amputate my leg?" When I told her yes, her eyes widened, and she said, "Oh, my God." But she didn't say it in her usual way as a means to express every reaction from excitement to disappointment: Omygod. This was the real thing. Every letter was enunciated. OH, MY GOD.

"Will I be able to run?" she asked later. "They will make something for you so that you can," I replied. She understood. There was an expression I had never seen on her face before, one no child should have to wear.

I've brought back a piece of toast and some tea, purchased quickly in the hospital coffee shop at the other end of the two-block-long corridor on the first floor. The uncooperative elevators annoy me, keeping me away from Alison. Though the hospital's policy toward parents who want to stay with their children is liberal, Bellevue doesn't make this easy. I can change and wash only in the visitors' washroom, a space about four feet square. A foot of this is taken up by an overflowing wastebasket, the contents of which I try to block from my mind. Later, when Charly arrives, I'll make my first trip home, to change finally from the azalea-pink dress I wore when the accident happened, on Thursday afternoon, to shower, and to get a change of clothes to bring back with me to the hospital.

"Have you been here all night?" Alison asks when she sees me eating beside her bed. The ladies-room wastebasket, the makeshift bed-chairs, the lack of sleep and shower, all disappear from my mind as I answer yes.

Sunday, July 28, 8:30 P.M.

Jonathan is here too. He cried when he came, but out in the hall, so that the tears would be shared only by us, not Alison. Peter did his crying when Charly told him of the accident, on the phone on Friday morning. Unable to talk to me afterward, he could only get on a plane and come as quickly as possible. Peter is still part of the family, just graduated from college, not yet into the world of business or entirely on his own. But Jonathan, though attached to us all, has been away over years and miles. He regrets the distance, one thousand miles, between us, between here and St. Louis where he lives. I understand his feelings. "I see Andrew again," he said, motioning his head toward the bed where Alison lies still and white. It's true. I'm reliving all the Andrew days too. I'm experiencing again, as I did then, what is really heartache. There is such a thing. The heart does ache. I don't know why. I know it's only a muscle, incapable of feeling. I know it should be brain-ache. But it's not. It's heartache, and it hurts.

Despite pain, despite morphine, Alison is trying hard to come back to the living. She remembers which people have come and stood by her bed here in intensive care, and she remembers whether it was morning or afternoon when they did. She remembered that she had a dentist's appointment tomorrow, Monday, and that she was to baby-sit next weekend. I had forgotten. I assured her I didn't have to cancel, that the whole town, the whole school, the whole temple congregation, indeed all the surrounding towns, had heard of her accident. It seemed to help her. One of her terrors must be coming home to face people a changed person, a different Alison. Now she knows she needn't tell them herself.

She ate this afternoon, to the delight of Roberta, the beautiful blue-eyed ICU nurse who was feeding her, and encouraged by her father, her brothers, and me. We are seeing improvement. Though she still feels hot all of the time, her lungs have cleared enough so that the breathing tube could be removed from her throat, and her pulse no longer appears ready to burst from her throat. But tomorrow she has to have surgery again, to close up the wound, which was left unfinished to allow it to drain. Then she'll have to come back from anesthesia all over again.

This afternoon she staved off asking for morphine for more than an hour because she wanted to stay awake to be with the boys. "I don't want to be out of it. I want to talk," she said. Finally, at two, the pain won over her need to be with us, but despite the drug, Alison kept herself awake for the next four hours. The fight was worth it. The three—sister and two brothers—began the type of banter they have established among themselves since Alison has become older: silly, senseless, and funny.

"What does the BHC on the hospital gown stand for?" she asked.

"Big hairy cucumber," Peter replied unhesitatingly. It brought a smile, the first, to Alison's lips.

This morning, Alison lay bewildered, her eyes dead, the spark gone, her depression an aura around her. I see how her mind is devouring her, just as mine does me and Charly's him. But with her brothers this afternoon, I felt in her a spark of strength, a need to regain control over her life, a need to laugh.

Our friends have come all day. They stand at the door of the ICU to see for themselves that this tragedy really happened. Most of them cry when I lead them out to the dingy waiting room outside the ICU.

The rabbi came and, standing close to Alison's bed, talked to her for some time. Later he told me what he had said to her: that the hand of God that held her so she might live was holding her now, too, to give her strength. *Shalom,* he told her, say that word to yourself when you need peace.

Alison asks repeatedly about the accident. Who was hit first, Jenni or she? How is Jenni? It worries me to tell her that Jenni will be all right, that she has a broken leg and crushed vertebrae that will respond well and permanently to a few weeks in a brace, but Alison seems relieved. It is the Alison I know who said, "Good" to my description of Jenni's far more minor injuries.

We have found out more about the accident, mostly through Jenni's dad, Warren, who now has the report of the police in Tenafly, where the accident happened. The driver is a Colombian national who speaks no English, is forty-six years old, and was driving someone else's car, his wife's or mother's. He was driving south toward Englewood, where he lives, on his way home from his work as a house painter. He was not drunk or under the influence of drugs, but that makes the accident all the more senseless. In a newspaper story that appeared today, he was quoted as saying that he thought Alison was going to cross the road. I could see this upset her. "Then it's my fault?" she asked. We assured her that even if the driver thought she was going to cross the road—and that seemed unlikely because there are no sidewalks on the other side either—it would have made no sense to steer toward the right, where Jenni was on the side of the telephone pole away from the street. Any driver, it seemed to me, would have steered into the middle or the left side of the street, even off the road on the other side, anything to avoid hitting a pedestrian. It was unmistakably his fault, and she must know that.

Jenni, who remembers everything about the accident, and who is suffering more from the pain of memory and fear than from her injuries, says that Alison had just stepped off the curb to go around the telephone pole, which stood a foot from the curb and between the girls. Jenni saw the car coming at them, saw the driver seemingly aim for them, and has continued to see his face behind the windshield. She and Alison were singing just before the accident and they were happy, Jenni told her parents.

Alison remembers nothing of singing or of being happy that day, but she now remembers having lunch with Jenni, hours before the accident. And, she remembers that when Heather expressed doubts about the weather for swimming on that Thursday morning, Alison agreed to cancel their date, glad for a chance to spend the day with Jenni, whom she hadn't seen for a while.

Monday, July 29, 12:05 A.M.

Alison wakes up, as she does each night. The blue, straightbacked chairs have begun to feel comfortable to me because they allow me to be at her side.

She is in pain, not terribly, but I wish I could take it away. Our nights are filled with my tears and her fears.

"Will I swim again?" she asks.

"Yes, next year."

I tell her about Dom Albanese, one of the high school counselors, who is looking for someone to teach her to ski again. It is repulsive to her. She doesn't know if she wants that. But I tell her she will have to try everything, and then when she succeeds, as she will, she'll feel happy once more. I hope I'm right.

I tell her that Dom said the whole town is praying for her. And I add they are crying for her, too, just like Daddy and Peter and Jonny. She says she hurts too much to cry.

We talk about the boy in the bed on the other side of my chair. His mother has the same sweet expression he has, but now her loveliness is masked by pain. Alison understands about his injuries, his paralysis. She tells me how sorry she feels for him. Alison hasn't changed. "It's better to be me than him," she says. "But it's better to be Jenni than me."

Another patient, six weeks old, a beautiful black baby with a cardiac problem and a foster mother and a twin brother to go home to, cries. Alison asks what is wrong with him. He is being suctioned, I say, as she was, to remove fluid from the lungs. "I didn't like that," she says. "I don't mind anything else, but I didn't like that."

She has said that the leg—the lost leg—wants to be on the bed. Now she says she wants to feel her knee—the stump—with her foot. I tell her she can, but she doesn't. Too soon.

Once again I am looking out into the dark from a hospital room, aching for my child. Last time, I was looking down at the wide street outside Babies Hospital, at the people crossing the street in the middle of the night, at the school across the way, the buildings with people without dying children in them. Now I look south, through narrow venetian-blind slats, at a bend in the East River Drive. The street lights look like planets in the blackness, their brightness unswerving. The headlights of the moving traffic, never ending even at this hour, are the stars, twinkling and moving through the slats. Shooting stars. Good luck stars.

A pediatrician has come to see Alison and at my urging tells her it's okay to cry. Alison's eyes fill a little, but the dull look remains.

Charly told his mother about Alison this morning. His sister and his stepbrother were there and they stayed with her so that Charly could come back here. She's a vibrant woman, but she has had a bad year, hurting herself severely after a fall and losing her brother. I have no strength left to give her solace. It couldn't have been easy for Charly, but he's strong when he's most needed. All through our lives together, I knew he could and would take on what I could not: the unpleasant jobs, like disposing of a dead bird, and the painful ones, like saying "amputate" and "leukemia" to people and like telling Jonathan of Andrew's death after we returned from the hospital that terrible April 13. It is he who has told everyone what happened. He has made the necessary phone calls, answered many more. I can barely talk about it. The only person to whom I actually said the words, "They had to amputate her leg," was my supervisor, on the first morning when I called my office to tell her what had happened. I haven't had to use the word since; Charly has said it over and over. But Charly reminds me that Alison is alive, and I remind Alison: she is alive, she is here, we are lucky. She understands she was near death.

My tears are always ready. The unexpected kindness of people I hardly know or whom I haven't seen for a very long time moves me most: a man in Cresskill, an acquaintance, offering to use his business limousine to bring carloads of kids to the hospital; the prayers, summoned by a decent and kind woman, mother of one of Andrew's friends, of a circle of thirty women belonging to the Methodist Church. Pray for strength for my child, good women. You are all saying *shalom*.

Monday, July 29, 7:30 A.M.

Morning is the hardest. The night is for Alison's questions and fears. Morning brings us sadness. This morning she saw the stump, in a bandage—the leg, she calls it—when Dr. Livingston came to change the dressing. Her depression was so deep that I couldn't reach her, even with tears. She's closing her eyes, not asleep, but trying to shut it out.

Though I felt nothing for Dr. Livingston the first night, I find I now depend on his coming, often in green operating-room garb, bare feet in wooden clogs, to put into perspective what is happening to us. He is sensitive to the needs of both of us. The first morning in the ICU, Saturday, he closed the curtain while he changed the dressing. I saw nothing and was

glad. Sunday morning he stood between me and the
stump as he dressed it, but not before I had seen the
sheets pulled back from the bandaged limb. I knew I
would have to face it sometime, and he accomplished
what I couldn't have made myself do alone. Similarly,
he led up to Alison's seeing her bandaged stump, as
she did this morning. But his attitude is one of healing—he tells her she is getting better, she will walk and
do many other things as she did before. He seems to
grow taller and wiser each time he enters the room.

I look at Alison's face as I stroke her brow. Her way
of lying there so despondent reminds me of the evening Andrew was diagnosed and how we had to leave
him at ten that night because the hospital did not allow
parents to stay with children. Only later, at the end,
when I fought, when I threatened to allow him to die
at home if I couldn't stay with him in the hospital, did
they relent and allow me to remain with him until he
died ten days later. I stroked the hair back from his
forehead too, that first night, over and over until we
had to leave him, knowing even in those first moments
that he would die.

But Alison won't die. There is nothing worse than
losing a child. One more moment, one less coopera-
tive person there to put a tourniquet on her, one less
gentle hand of God, and she would have been taken
from us too. I need not once again scream and scream
and scream a lost child's name without a sound coming from me. Just a name bouncing off nothingness,
echoing back to me, dying finally in silence, as the
child did.

Four

EIGHT NORTH

Monday, July 29, 9:00 A.M.

The ICU nurse tells me an orderly will come soon to take Alison to the operating room. I knew this operation had to be; nevertheless, I see it as a setback to her recovery. She is in a lot of pain today all over her battered body, but she's finally off the breathing tube and oxygen and the post-operative misery. Now she will have to start all over.

Monday, July 29, 2:00 P.M.

The driver is indigent, and there is little chance of monetary recovery beyond his minimum insurance coverage. Furthermore—the police say—he drove "carelessly," a minor offense, but not "recklessly," with intent to inflict harm. But I could conceive of a punishment for him that would constitute justice: remand him to work in a children's hospital for a given time. He would never again drive as he did, endangering a pedestrian, a child. If, preparatory to Alison's surgery this morning, he had seen a strong nurse and a robust orderly straining to move this eighty-five-pound girl from bed to stretcher, trying to roll her gently, he would have felt Alison's pain. Everything hurts her. It was agonizing for her to be moved, rolled and lifted, but she never cried out, only grimaced and finally groaned quietly. She hasn't cried yet, about anything.

I stood back as the stretcher bearing Alison was wheeled from the ICU, but the attendant motioned me to come along and said I could wait on the surgical floor with Alison until she was taken into the operating room. Though sedated, Alison was awake and aware. I was glad to be with her when she needed me, glad that people cared, about Alison, about me, perhaps about themselves and their own feelings at seeing Alison's bandaged stump and her tight control.

Jonathan and Peter weren't here at ten when the orderly came to take Alison to surgery. Each wanted to see her once more before he left, Jon later this morning for St. Louis and, this evening, Peter for Dartmouth. When they raced into the ICU moments after Alison and I had left, they were devastated to see her gone; Jon, especially, assuming he wouldn't see her again for a long time. As Alison and I waited outside the operating room, we heard a commotion near the elevator. A young resident, seeing the boys' distress at having missed Alison, had escorted them upstairs to the surgical floor and was now pointing us out to them.

There we were: Alison on a stretcher, trying to fight the sedative; I beside her, wishing it were I on the stretcher; and her brothers distracting us with silly stories, jokes, and pictures of Peter's two kittens, Hamlet and Ophelia, pictures he had rushed to pick up from the photo store, the reason he and Jon arrived late. After a while, I persuaded the boys to allow Alison to doze, and they sat on the floor and read the paper. But they were there, and Alison knew it. It was a long wait, over an hour, an hour that went by in fewer than sixty minutes because we were together. No one ever let me stay with Andrew except during the routine weekly examinations by a doctor who seemed to care only about the disease, not the patient. I couldn't stay with Andrew when he most needed me, not even when he had to have spinal taps and I could hear him behind the closed door crying out despite himself. Afterward, wan and hurting, he rode home beside me, staring ahead as Alison now does, enmeshed in terrible thoughts. I had not even been able to hold his hand. And he was only eight years old.

Now the boys are gone. Peter will be here again next weekend; Jon cried as he said good-bye to me. It is expensive to come from the Midwest, and his job is demanding and time-consuming. He doesn't know when he'll be back. He feels like a visitor. Peter and Alison are very close. They share memories. Jon has been away eleven years, since he left for Washington University in St. Louis at eighteen. He's torn between living in St. Louis, where he has friends and spends his weekends white-water canoeing, and being nearer here, where he has family. He's jealous of Peter, he admits, for his easygoing disposition, his successes, his relationship with Alison. Jonathan is different, a darker, more intense person. Peter is light and optimistic, joyous and self-assured, as is— was—Alison. Jon will have to work out his conflicts himself. To his plaint that he is not part of Peter and Alison's memories, I tell him that he was part of earlier memories, memories of Andrew, which he shares with Charly and me, and of which his siblings are not a part.

"But it's a new life now; I'm not part of that," he says.

"I feel," I answer, "as if Dad and I have lived three lives: with Andrew, the one you share; Alison's childhood, which Peter shares; and our changed life from here on, which perhaps we'll all share, because she'll need us all."

Monday, July 29, 4:15 P.M.

Just a couple of hours have passed. Charly has come back, needed in his office but unable to work, anxious about the outcome of the operation. Alison is in the recovery room, and again we were allowed to see her for a few moments. We are sitting by her bed in the ward where she'll be, but Peter, who was in the recovery room with us, asked to stay with Alison longer.

That act of kindness, though, may be the last rule we will see bent for some time, or ever, in Bellevue Hospital. When Charly and I carried Alison's and my few belongings past the elevators, from the pediatrics ICU on Eight South to pediatrics on Eight North, we stopped at the nurses' station for directions to her designated bed and encountered the ward's enforcer of rules, the head nurse.

As Charly and I followed her down the corridor, her sturdy legs hammering out the path she has surely trodden for a lifetime, her white dress swishing at her knees from the power of her stride, her tiny nurses' cap perched on her gray hair, I sensed her feelings about parents who ask questions and show concern for their child's comfort. This was her territory. She would brook no interference.

"This," she said, pointing to a bed with its mattress adjusted to the highest point, the position for receiving a patient on a stretcher, "will be your daughter's bed." She pulled a sheet of paper forward on the dresser beside the bed. "And these," she added, "are the rules. They are not to be broken." With that, her eyes tightened, making them yet smaller. She took a pencil and forcefully circled one section of the printed form, highlighting that portion.

"Only two visitors at any time," she read the circled words, using the point of the pencil to reiterate the rule, "including the parents. Visitors between the ages of fourteen and seventeen may visit only between the hours of four P.M. and seven P.M." She looked at us. "There will be no exceptions," she said, pursing her lips.

How did this woman know that I would do everything possible to fight those rules? Alison's friends, who I believe may become the most important part of her recovery, can't get here by 4:00 P.M., much less get here so as to leave by 7:00 P.M. They all have summer jobs. From New Jersey they might at best get here by

7:00 P.M. And how can I ask them to come only two at a time? It is a long trip; there is no public transportation that takes them far down on the East Side of Manhattan where Bellevue Hospital is located. They must wait for rides from parents or friends. Most don't drive yet, and almost none are eighteen years old, the age required for driving in New York City.

"The Wicked Witch of Eight North," I mumbled under my breath to Charly, though I was intimidated. Now I can't wait for Alison to come down from surgery and awaken sufficiently so that she can meet the head nurse. Despite my annoyance, I realize with joy that Alison is alive; she may have lost a leg, but she is here, and soon I can share things with her again, like laughing about the Wicked Witch.

Monday, July 29, 10:15 P.M.

I am alone again, Alison sleeping beside me. To write, I must have all the overhead fluorescent lights blazing. It doesn't matter tonight; Alison is oblivious to them and to almost everything else except the need to sleep off the anesthesia, and there is no one in the room with us. Tomorrow I'll have Charly bring me a small desk lamp so that I can write and read without disturbing others. This will be my home for several weeks, four according to Dr. Livingston when he saw us this evening. My bed will remain two blue chairs, just as in the ICU, though I had been led to believe there were cots available for parents sleeping with their children in the ward. There are no cots, says the Wicked Witch; there are not even two chairs. "You are entitled to use one chair," she stated, even before I asked about the use of two. The woman reads minds. I don't care; I've taken another chair from beside an empty bed so that I can lie across two. There is no one else in this large room meant for four patients. I had no difficulty finding the other chair.

Alison's room now faces north on the East River Drive, overlooking the 34th Street Heliport at the edge of the river. The view is magnificent; to the right is Brooklyn across a bend in a wide part of the river, and to the left is Manhattan seen looking north from 28th Street, where the hospital is located, into the tangle of towering buildings. At night the graceful spire of the Chrysler Building, lit up in its rings of art deco elegance, shows behind the other lighted skyscrapers. I can see where the hospital got its name: *belle vue.*

Warren and Earlyn Earabino, Jenni's parents, came here this evening. Because we are no longer in the ICU, they were the first visitors who have sat with us beside Alison's bed. Until now we were forced to talk with friends in the dingy pediatrics waiting room, its black and white tile floor permanently encrusted with dirt, its upright ashtrays spilling the effluence of distraught parents: crushed paper cups, shredded tissues, stubbed-out cigarette butts.

Though Alison kept her eyes closed throughout their visit, she knew the Earabinos were here. They spoke quietly of the accident, the senselessness of it, and of the injustice of the driver's life continuing unaltered because he is indigent, stopping hope of a lawsuit against him, and because he was not charged with reckless driving. What tragic fate, we asked ourselves, brought two girls to a specific spot at a specific time— the same instant as that blue Ford?

"They were happy. They were two happy little girls having a good day and walking home together," Earlyn said softly. "They were singing. Did you know they were singing? Jenni had bought the record 'Border-line,' and they were singing the song because they were nearing the border of Tenafly and Cresskill."

She suggested I ask Alison tomorrow whether she remembers singing, thinking it would bring back some memories of that day. Alison asks for more information about the day, the hours before the accident; she remembers only snatches of July 25.

The visit was difficult for the Earabinos. Earlyn talks of Jenni's injuries, and I know she is thinking of Alison's too, but I cannot think of Jenni's injuries. Jenni cried bitterly, her father says, about having to wear a back brace, about having it show under her clothes. But in a couple of weeks she'll be walking, and a few weeks after that she'll be fine. I don't wish Jenni more injuries; she has all she can handle. I only wish Alison fewer injuries, but my wishes are useless. I do care about Jenni's fears and sorrow. She remembers the car coming at her. She remembers the driver's face behind the windshield. That must be unbearable. And, an exuberant and loving girl, a giving and caring friend, she must be going through hell, imagining Alison's injuries, knowing there was nothing she could do to help, remembering that only inches kept her from the same fate.

The two have been friends for five years, since

Jenni's older sister, Liz, began dating Peter in high school. I don't know if Peter and Liz's relationship will last much longer even after all these years; I think it's coming apart slowly this summer. But the younger two, the girls, have had a warm and fun-filled friendship. Together with Linda Rosenberg, who has been Alison's friend since kindergarten, they have shared many good hours as a threesome with disparate personalities. Linda is quiet, reserved, cool. Jenni is tumultuous, flamboyant, emotional. Alison, a mix of both, holds them together. Yet, I heard that Linda cried, with her parents, for hours after hearing of the accident. And it is Linda who is taking care of our animals every evening, giving up her free time to relieve our minds of that burden. But Jenni is the one to whom Alison will have to reach out, because Jenni's pain surely extends beyond the crushed vertebrae and the hairline fracture in her leg.

I am tired. I sleep, for short periods and not deeply, but that's good, because I'm aware of Alison's every movement. In any case, I awaken each hour to shift in the chair, resting my head first on one metal armrest and then the other. A small pillow from home cushions my head, making the chairs more precious than a luxury suite in a hotel. They keep me near Alison.

Tuesday, July 30, 5:15 A.M.

The sun is coming up over the East River. The red light of early morning washes all the buildings in its hue, touching the homely factories in Brooklyn just as it does the stately high-rises in Manhattan. The sun is coming up, and my child is alive and beautiful. I believe there is *shalom*.

Tuesday, July 30, 8:30 A.M.

Yesterday morning, in the ICU, the nurse asked me if I wanted to wash Alison because I'd be doing it when she is moved to the ward. Alison was in such pain that I was afraid to touch her and asked the nurse to take care of her while I watched and learned. I was called to the phone, and I never did watch that morning.

This morning I had no choice. A basin was brought with some soft paper towels and I was told to bathe Alison. As long as she is not moved, she's all right, so I rolled her over as little as I possibly could. But I couldn't contain my shock. Her body, from the waist down to the top of the bandage on the amputated leg, which was as far as I could see on her left side, and to the knee of the right leg, is black. Not black and blue. Black. Black, as though someone had spilled matte charcoal-colored paint on her. This is where the pain is. The broken pelvis. The broken hip. And those hideously injured muscles and tissues and skin that cover them.

I could almost see the outline of the center of the Ford's hood that smashed into her. On Saturday, as I drove home through Tenafly, I saw the car parked at a garage. I couldn't believe the dent in the front of it. A deep v, two feet in from where the front of the car should be, has made the car forever unusable. It waits to be junked, its presence testimony of that

July 25 impact. Even that metal wreck, even the sight of the telephone pole, split in half where the impact occurred and propped up now by a hastily erected auxiliary pole, were not as shocking to me as Alison's maimed body.

Tuesday, July 30, 1:00 P.M.

Unlike Tennessee Williams's Blanche du Bois, I am not dependent on the kindness of strangers, but I am moved by them to the point where I cannot even get out the words "thank you."

On Saturday afternoon, leaving Charly with Alison, I planned to go home for a short time with Peter. When Peter and I got to the parking garage, we realized that between us we didn't have half the money we needed to pay for the several hours' parking charge. I was loath to go back to Charly for the money because all I wanted was to get home and back as quickly as possible. The attendant insisted he was not permitted to take a check, nor could he accept an IOU. This, finally, was more than I could bear, and we told him why we didn't want to take the time to go back to the hospital to get the money.

"I'll lay out the money for you myself," he said.

Sunday morning I walked back to the garage to repay the attendant, but my voice choked and my eyes filled as I tried to thank him. I think he understood. Don't anyone ever again tell me about the bad people in New York City. They're there, but so are the good ones, and we are meeting them.

The rabbi was here earlier, and I think his visit

helped Alison. Her voice was stronger, less subdued, after he left. She talks very little, just a sentence here or there, but he said she talked to him, and he to her, about fear and pain and God. He is going away next week, on vacation. I'm afraid of his going. He listens, and I can talk to him.

He brought with him a collage made by several of Alison's friends—Linda, Heather, Heather's sister Erica, and a few others. The youngsters pasted on photographs of themselves and Alison sharing past good times, together with cartoons and balloon quotes over the pictures. The sayings spell out: "We love you." "We will stand by you." "Be strong." "Don't give up." "You are not alone." And it's all done with humor. Though Alison hasn't the strength to hold the large cardboard collage, she wants me to hold it so that she can study it intently. The girls have been selective in their choice and cropping of photographs: there are no full shots of Alison. A wax rose, adding a third dimension to the collage, covers half of a pose, where Alison's legs would be.

Just a while ago the first flowers arrived. One arrangement was from our friends, and Alison was pleased, but two others, twin arrangements from twins she worked with this summer at Tammy Brook, made her say over and over, "Wasn't it nice of Sean and Nicole to send the flowers? Aren't they pretty? Wasn't it nice of them?" I am grateful to this unknown pair. They sparked a light in Alison's eyes.

She isn't ready yet to see her friends, and I doubt whether they would be ready to see her as she is now, but I know how important they will be to her.

Wednesday, July 31, 7:00 A.M.

Compared to everything else, not being able to urinate for more than a day since the catheter was removed after the surgery on Monday is only a small indignity. Alison tried all day yesterday, and finally at 10:30 in the evening the doctor woke me to tell me he would have to catheterize her again. It gave her relief.

I had slept deeply on my two chairs from the time Charly left at 8:30 P.M. until the doctor woke me, and I slept again until the nurse woke me at 4:30 A.M. to try to get Alison to urinate. It didn't work. The pain is terrible each time Alison must be moved so that she can use a bedpan. She has to clutch me standing at the side of the bed as the nurse rolls or lifts her. Still, she no longer says, as she did in the ICU, that everything hurts. But at 4:30 she was in pain. She never cries out, never cries, never, never complains, just whispers, "I have pain." I tried to get medicine for her. It had been changed from morphine in the ICU to Demerol here on the ward. We waited forty-five minutes, all the time Alison showing her pain only by asking quietly, politely where the nurse was. I was told the nurse was on break—forty-five minutes—but when she came she gave Alison two pills—Tylenol with codeine—and they worked. Alison went back to sleep, as did I, until I woke with a start not believing I had fallen back asleep until 6:30. I can't do that in my own bed.

It's harder on Charly than it is on me. We're financially secure because of him, and because of that and because of the help and cooperation I am getting from my company, I'm able to take a leave of absence to be with Alison all the time. Caring for her eases my torment and puts me in her world. Charly has more than three hours of driving each day—to New Brunswick each morning, here to the hospital in the early afternoon, and finally home at night. When he comes to stay with Alison while I go home, he sits quietly by her bed. I then drive as quickly as possible and, once home, take a shower and change my clothes, perhaps do the laundry and clean up a little, and then speed back down the East River Drive to my real home, my spot in the hospital next to Alison. When I get back, we make sure Alison is asleep and then we try to force ourselves to eat dry-tasting sandwiches in the hospital coffee shop. When Charly finally leaves, because I see his exhaustion, it's nine o'clock. He goes home alone to five upset animals. One of them, our dog Heidi, who has Addison's disease, which is aggravated by stress, is letting out her frustrations by leaving him unwanted gifts all over the house. And he goes home to phone calls, endless phone calls. Every message, usually left with Linda while she is in the house taking care of the animals, says, "Call immediately." It is difficult—and tiring—for him to talk about Alison. On the other hand, it helps him to know how much people care.

But we've gone through all this before. When Andrew was hospitalized the last time, the ten days before he died, I finally did stay with him, night and day. Peter was not even three then, and I was torn between being home with my oldest son and with my baby, who also needed me, or being with Andrew, who would soon know nothing more. I didn't have to choose. Though I believed that we had to go on living our lives for the children who would grow up with memories of the death, I had to be with Andrew at the end.

Charly and I coped the same way then. I slept on a chair in Andrew's hospital room. In the afternoon, Charly came and stayed with him while I went home. Our baby-sitter, Tess Reilly, who gave up more than a year and a half of her own life during Andrew's illness, would go home to care for her own family while I got Peter ready for bed and gave him and Jonny dinner. Tess returned; I went back to Babies Hospital; Charly came home; and Tess could again go to her own home until early the next morning, when Charly left for work.

This time I have no conflict. There is no other child but Alison. She is my only concern. And I have no doubt as to the necessity of my being here. There is not even a bell at Alison's bed for her to call the nurse were I not here. She is at the other end of the hall from the nurses' station and would be unable to call out loud enough if she needed something. The nurses don't come even when I ask them to. This morning I asked one nurses' aide whether she would help me roll Alison to her side. I can't do this alone because it hurts her so to be moved, but it is important because she gets uncomfortable lying in one position only. The woman turned around on the stool where she perched, turned her back to me, and said, "Not my patient." There are a few caring nurses and nurses' aides here, but they are rare and very much appreciated.

There are two other girls in the room now, each twelve years old and each in for short stays, one overnight for surgery on her foot and the other for bronchitis. Neither has a parent with her, so I still have my two chairs. Alison would like to be friendly and looks over at them frequently. But she's too weak to talk above a whisper, much less across the room. She has just begun to be propped up a little in bed from the completely flat position she was in because of the broken hip. And neither of the girls speaks English.

Alison is so quiet. She thinks so much. How can I blame her? My mind never stops. What must be going on in hers? Some of her thoughts come out in the things she says. "I'm going to have trouble walking when I get old, because I'll have trouble even when I'm young." "What will I look like?" "What will happen when I go back to school?" "Will I ever have a boyfriend?" I imagine that there are many more fledgling fears that will grow to be vultures in her mind.

"I'm sixteen and a half today," she remembers. "I could have gotten my driver's permit today."

Wednesday, July 31, 8:00 A.M.

Dr. Livingston made his visit, as he does each morning at 7:30 and told Alison she has to start fighting. "Yell and scream and punch me if I'm hurting you," he said, "but don't just lie there and take it. Fight back." She was better after he left, stronger, responsive.

Wednesday, July 31, 10:00 A.M.

It's just two hours later. Alison is much better. She again studied her friends' collage, but this time instead of just staring at it, taking it all in in silence, she laughed about the messages within it and the memories the photographs evoked. She wants to have her hair washed. She wants to have her nails done. She is beginning to live again.

Part of the renewed light in her eyes surely comes from the cards that are beginning to reach us and from the flowers that are beginning to brighten the room. They all show people's concern for her. She knows it. She needs it.

Alison had her first encounter with stupid remarks made to the disabled, from a nurse. The young nurse, in a hurry while trying to change Alison's position and receiving no active help from Alison, commanded, "Push with both legs." I glared at her. She repeated her order.

I spat out, "Miss!" I couldn't say "Nurse." "Do you know why she's here?" She apologized, said she hadn't known. What do they talk about when they're making rounds at the time they change shifts? It was okay, though. I told Alison we had just met up with the first of what will be many hurting remarks. For a moment I wanted to hit the nurse, I said, and then I dismissed it, no longer angry. I got over it. Alison didn't get mad—but I wish she had.

Wednesday, July 31, 9:30 P.M.

I can barely write anymore, I'm so tired. It's not because I'm doing nothing all day, or because I get no exercise. The whole overwhelming emotionality of it all is finally washing over me, like ocean waves engulfing me, which was the way I saw my feelings of helplessness and hopelessness when Andrew was sick. But Alison is alive, and she's going to stay alive. No matter how maimed she is, she will go on living.

Five

REALITY BEGINS

Thursday, August 1, 11:30 A.M.

One week. Last week at this time I was at the office
trying to juggle my current project so it could move to
its next stage. I did think of Alison periodically, even
though my preoccupation was with my work. I thought
of her with the inner pleasure I usually felt when her
image penetrated busy minutes: that she was happy
and well.

Alison *was* happy and well at this time last week.
Jenni's father had just given the girls a ride to
Tenafly, just two miles south of Cresskill, but with its
own distinctive character, very different from that of
our town of eight thousand. Jenni and Alison were
planning to have lunch at the Clinton Inn coffee
shop and then to immerse themselves in the bargains
and baubles of a sidewalk sale. Storekeepers cram
their wares on tables and racks on the sidewalk in
front of their stores, hoping to sell as much merchan-
dise as possible in the two or three summer days of
the sale's duration. The streets are closed to cars. It

is a scene of brightly colored hanging garments and tables piled with makeup, shoes, linens, costume jewelry, toys, T-shirts, children's clothes, women's clothes, men's clothes. People fill the broad main street, tugging at little children, calling to each other when a treasure is spied, admiring each other's purchases, greeting neighbors whom they haven't seen during the cold winter months, pulling out wallets as wonders are spied. It is a suburban scene, but it is derived from Arab markets, New York's Lower East Side, and the bodegas on the city's Upper East Side. Jenni bought a record; Alison considered buying earrings and then decided against them. She dawdled over the purchase of eye shadow, debating over this shade or that. They met friends, stopped and talked, then met others, stopped again. Each moment spent or saved was bringing them inexorably to the instant of impact.

Thursday, August 1, 1:00 P.M.

I did what I resolved to do. Leaving Alison alone, I hurried to the main floor to find the proper hospital administrator; I was determined to have the visitors' rules relaxed for Alison. Going from person to person to find someone who could help me, I was told to speak to the head nurse. Obviously, that was not going to help; she is the problem, not the solution. After half an hour of knocking on wrong doors or closed doors, I found a person who would listen to me and who agreed that (1) I was not a hysterical mother, unreasonably looking for special favors for her spoiled child, (2) having young people visit her would be a healing element for Alison, (3) allowing visits from two people only, and only during the designated hours, would create a hardship for us and for them, (4) bending the rules would be made easier by Alison's being alone in the room most of the time, and (5) Alison's age, older than the other girls on the pediatric floor at that time, was a factor in her needing the support of her friends at a traumatic time in her life. The order was signed: four visitors at a time and until 9:30 P.M. It will be sent to the head nurse.

Memories of Andrew engulfed me again, threatening to undermine my controlled presentation to the administrator. In October 1964, after having gone through three weeks of hospitalization after leukemia was diagnosed in July, after having taken huge doses of cortisone, which made his cheeks fatten into the typical moon face associated with the drug and his abdomen swell to give him a pearlike shape, after having gotten past that and onto another drug, vincristine, which made his hair fall out and caused him to lose all the "cortisone" weight he had gained and then some, so that he was pale and thin with dark circles under his eyes, he was well enough to go back to school more than four weeks after the term had started. On November 1 he would be eight and eligible to become a Cub Scout, his deepest wish. The Boy Scout rule against wearing any part of the uniform before induction was waived by the scoutmaster, and, Andrew wore the precious Cub Scout cap one month

49

early so that he could cover his balding head when school began.

That loss of hair hadn't come easily to him. When this handsome boy with the chiseled features, so fastidious that even at seven he combed his hair carefully, discovered a handful of hair in his hand, he howled so like a knifed animal that the sound brought me running from the other end of the street where I was walking the dog, certain he had been mortally harmed. It crushed his spirit beyond even the many other indignities he had to undergo and the pain he had to endure.

He went off to school that first day with his little blue cap on his head. That afternoon the man who was then the school's principal called to say that the rules required boys to remove head coverings while in the building. He knew Andrew had leukemia. He also knew his rules. I drove to the school prepared to battle. For half an hour I described Andrew's illness to the principal, described its certain fatal outcome, the suffering that Andrew had already borne and would surely continue to bear, the nature of the drugs available to create a remission period for a child with leukemia, and the necessity of preserving Andrew's dignity, even in the face of baldness at the age of seven, and his willingness to come to school where the other children would see him in that condition.

"But we can't make any exceptions, Mrs. Lehmann," the principal asserted, bringing his fingers together in a spire formation before him. "If we do, the other children will expect to be permitted to do the same thing."

"Andrew is an exception," I retorted. "And, please God, I hope he remains the only exception."

I won my case.

Thursday, August 1, 2:00 P.M.

Dr. Livingston told Alison she must get out of bed today, and late this morning the burliest, and also the kindest and gentlest, of the pediatric interns lifted her into a wheelchair that I had padded heavily with pillows. Two of the nurses had earlier tried to help her out of bed, but the pain was so severe that I suggested they get a doctor. With one movement he lifted her from the bed and into the chair, where she sat slumped and wan for almost an hour until the young intern returned to release her from exile and hoist her back onto the bed she yearned for. Now she is sleeping, as she does much of the day.

Today is a Swiss national holiday. My mother is in her native Switzerland for the summer, not planning to return until the end of August. We've decided not to tell her anything now. She wasn't well when she left several weeks ago, and she needs the time there with her relatives to regain her strength. It's a painful decision, one we made only after assurances by both the rabbi and the hospital psychiatrist that we were not wrong. Telling her now would surely bring her back on a lonely and grieving flight, and it would not help us at all. Once divorced and once widowed, she depends on her relationship with me, her only child. Neither Charly nor I have anything to give to anyone except Alison right now.

Thursday, August 1, 10:00 P.M.

Alison asked about prostheses, how they work, how they look. I didn't know. She was quiet for a while and then said, "I think I'd like to see Wayne now."

I called Eileen Siegmann at 3:00 P.M., telling her that Alison would like to see Wayne any time it was convenient for him. He was at the hospital in half an hour, his white shirt setting off his open, tanned face, his briefcase swinging with each tilting step he takes. They are quick steps, sure steps, but his limp is pronounced. I'm sure the identification with Wayne has caused Alison to delay this meeting until now. All week, mention of Wayne has deepened Alison's depression: her eyes became more lifeless, she pulled away from me. But today she was ready.

Wayne talked alone with Alison for over an hour about his own amputation at age fifteen. She has been too weak until now to tolerate more than a few minutes' conversation. Afterward, though she was tired, she said it was good to talk to him. I could see she was more relaxed, as though she had faced something that had preyed on her.

Wayne's visit was good for me, too. As I drove Wayne back to Cresskill, I was able to ask him questions: How do you take a shower? What do you do about socks? (For some reason, I kept thinking of her needing only one sock at a time, but of course his answer reminded me that Alison will have a prosthesis someday and will not always be one-legged.) What happens if she remembers the moment of impact, as the hospital psychiatrist keeps insisting she must? How will the other kids feel toward her? What does it feel like to be seen without a prosthesis, like at the town pool? How do you swim in the ocean? What does it mean to live the life of someone handicapped, disabled? I could barely fit my queries into the hour's drive home. Of most comfort, because he had said it to Alison also, was Wayne's telling me that he immediately had determined that he would never allow his amputation to serve as an excuse for not participating in anything. "If that's the way I acted," he said, "then I figured the other kids would treat me like everyone else too. And they did."

I told Wayne the story Dom Albanese had related to me. On hearing of Alison's accident, Dom had said to his wife, Bonnie, "Now is when I wish I knew where to find Wayne Siegmann. I've lost touch with him. He could help Alison so much." "Dom," Bonnie answered, "Wayne lives right across the street from Alison!"

My initial call to Eileen this afternoon had answered one of my unacknowledged questions. Without a prompt from me, she said, "I've never thought of Wayne as having one leg or two. I love him as a person, not because of his legs." I hope Alison will hear words like that from a man who loves her.

Andrea and Audrey were here this evening—the first of Alison's friends to visit. Audrey has known her since nursery school; they attended religious school together through confirmation. Andrea is a more recent friend, a happy, warm person she met in summer camp three years ago and who happens to live just minutes from us. I met them outside Alison's room and tried to warn them that they would see the outline of the stump; they were not to be shocked. If they were, they didn't flinch. They were sensitive and loving. "We love you, Alison," they said. "Don't ever give up; we'll stick by you." All the right words. Alison was quiet, letting them talk but listening intently. They have been begging for days to come and see her, but I've put them off until now. I think they would have been too frightened by Alison's condition and Alison would have been too tired and depressed before this.

Sometimes the four-bed room Alison is in has one other girl in it, occasionally two, often none. The only other girl now is thirteen, and from what I can make out from her mother's broken English, the doctors are having difficulty diagnosing her problem. She looks the way Andrew did when he was on cortisone, and though the girl is shy and I can't get to know her because of the language barrier, I feel a kinship with her.

There is little English spoken here. Most of the pediatric patients are Hispanics—all apparently poor, and they rarely get visitors. Alison's room, overflowing with flowers, cards, posters, and teddy bears is an anomaly. The other rooms are devoid of even a card. I ache for the other children, not because they don't have the flowers and teddy bears, though I wish they did, but because they don't have what those gifts represent. For Alison they are the ties to her previous life, visible evidence of the support system that has been built up through sixteen years of her life, twenty-four years of our being involved congregants in our temple, and thirty-one years of living in Cresskill, a town and its people I embraced by spending fifteen years running a weekly preschool story hour and by serving as president of the elementary and high school PTAs. We are not alone, not any of us, least of all Alison.

Even the hospital—a city hospital—has been a source of comfort. Except for the cockroaches that swarm in the bathroom attached to Alison's room and to which I'm becoming accustomed, and except for some lackadaisical nurses who would regard helping a child that is "not their responsibility for the day" an imposition, this city within a city is a place of warmth and kindness.

There is much to appreciate. The compassionate people who have been so good to us here. The many people outside the hospital who wrote to us—some daily—to say all they are feeling. The gifts of flowers that now number two dozen, the teddy bears, cuddly stuffed dogs and comical animals, even fabric fruits and satin hot-air balloons with tiny gondolas floating beneath them: each is important to Alison's recovery and, as evidence of love, to Charly and me. Additionally, the management at Tammy Brook Country Club has started a fund in Alison's name, distributing to every one of its hundreds of members a flier asking for donations for "that sweet petite brunette who worked in the snack bar." How can I ever write all these thank-you cards? Warren Earabino, who told me of Tammy Brook's fund, suggests I have something printed. But

I *want* to write; my heart overflows into my pen as I think of people's sympathy. I am writing letters with my child beside me. Not like the last time, when I wrote thank-you cards for sympathy for a child we buried.

Friday, August 2, 6:00 A.M.

After my initial distress at having Alison on a pediatric floor surrounded by noisy, seemingly well and apparently hyperactive children racing up and down the halls, and having to abide by visiting rules meant for this ward, I asked Dr. Livingston about moving her to an adult ward. Surely the rules would not be as stringent there, I said, and there would be no rigid head nurse to enforce them. He recommended that Alison remain here, describing her as sixteen-going-on-seventeen, rather than sixteen-going-on-thirty, an impression he drew immediately in the emergency room before the surgery, when she wasn't saying a word. Alison has taken her time growing up. She has been able to take her time . . . until now.

Friday, August 2, 8:15 A.M.

Now there is a trapeze across Alison's bed, a horizontal metal bar that extends from head to foot with a large triangle suspended from it just above Alison's arms. She is to pull up on the triangle to achieve a sitting position in the bed, thereby strengthening her arms in preparation for the use of crutches. I hadn't thought of crutches. I haven't really thought of any form of locomotion for Alison, but I understand now that crutches will be a permanent part of her life. Any time she is not wearing her prosthesis—in the morning before she is dressed, at night as she is going to bed—she will have to be on crutches. It is a new thought for me, and for her.

When the trapeze was installed above her bed, Dr. Livingston grew even taller in Alison's and my eyes. He had ordered the trapeze yesterday and gave instructions for erecting it. When he arrived this morning the metal poles had been delivered, but no one had attempted to install the trapeze. It's the only time I've seen him angry. But his anger was transposed into a little boy's pleasure in playing with his Erector Set. Giving orders like a construction foreman, for he always travels with his retinue of resident surgeons, he had the trapeze up in minutes, climbing on the bed, from side to side and end to end, handing a pole to a doctor here, setting another pole into a headpost there, all the time with Alison looking on wide-eyed beneath him. The trapeze was up, he was evidently well satisfied with his work and with its potential for Alison's recovery, and he bounded out of the room expecting big changes in Alison because of the trapeze.

Friday, August 2, 10:15 A.M.
There is something about a hospital stay that turns your thoughts around. When your parameters are a hospital bed, two chairs, a TV, and a few shopping bags of belongings, it enables you to pour every resource

into recovery and moving forward. The first few days I could focus only on the past, on that lovely, lively, slim-legged teenager so full of active promise. As the days pass here I find I am beginning to focus on the future—on Alison, still a lovely, lively teenager, full of active promise.

Alison, too, is focusing on the future. With fear, of course, but with acceptance. Maybe the word is resignation.

There were friends here much of yesterday. For the most part Alison is withdrawn, unwilling to enter into any conversation, tired. But I can see her looking forward to strength.

Friday, August 2, 11:30 A.M.

Alison was taken to the hospital's rehabilitation unit this morning. It was only the second time she sat up, and she was tired even before we got her wheelchair down there. I was allowed to accompany her, and I silently praised again this hospital's relaxed rules, those not enforced by our head nurse. In error the attendant pushed the wheelchair into a physical therapy room crowded with elderly, disabled people, silently performing tasks to bring back wasted minds and bodies. One man pulled on a scrap of fabric, again and again, to strengthen weakened arm muscles. Alison's chair was left at the side of the room. I stood beside her. For the first time tears rolled down her cheeks. "Are you thinking, 'How did we get here?' " I asked through my own tears. She nodded. I wished the scene were as unreal as it looked.

When the attendant finally wheeled her to the right room, one in which people with injuries and ailments exercised, had limp muscles pushed and pulled, and learned to walk, Alison hunched down in the wheelchair, watching quietly. An old man wearing undershorts was perched at the edge of a cot, a brown shoe and a gray sock on one foot, the knee of the other leg hanging over the edge of the bed, ending abruptly in a stump.

"I wish I had my knee," Alison whispered.

It was too soon to begin rehabilitation today, one of the therapists told us. We waited for a rehabilitation doctor, who would check her condition and plan for rehabilitation at Bellevue. Alison was disappointed by his evaluation. Because of the gravity of her injuries she will have to go to a rehabilitation center for about four weeks after the four weeks at Bellevue. She had hoped to complete the second part of her hospital recuperation at Englewood Hospital where her friends could visit her more easily. I wish I could cheer up Alison, but I am as depressed as she is.

But I have to think of what is already behind us. Janis Weiss, the wife of the couple who was with us the first night and with whom I am most often in touch, told me she called to thank the young medical student who was one of the first people at the scene of the accident and who reacted quickly to the need for a tourniquet. And Dom Albanese, the school guidance counselor, told me of his friend John Tessaro, who appeared at the scene of the accident moments later. Seeing Alison lying prostrate and seeing the extent of her injuries, John was certain at first that she was dead.

In the dust and blood around her, he said, they assumed she was a grown woman. It was only when they turned her over that they realized there were still signs of life and that this was a young girl. Nearby, Jenni was sitting up, screaming. Her screams had attracted the two drivers because the crumpled blue Ford hid the girls from view. I wonder whether Jenni saw Alison's leg and was screaming about that. She doesn't remember.

Friday, August 2, 8:30 P.M.

This afternoon was better than this morning, but not because Alison felt stronger; she didn't. She lay very still in her bed after her pediatric intern friend moved her back from her wheelchair to the bed. But she had welcome visitors. Dom Albanese, concerned about Alison, anxious to help, trying to pave whatever path Alison has to travel, has asked repeatedly what he can do. Yesterday, when I spoke to him, I told him how much playing the minor lead parts in school plays had meant to Alison during her freshman and sophomore years. "I think it's on her mind, Dom: 'What's going to happen to the plays? Will I still be in them?'" Today, he stood outside her room with Al McLaughlin, the school's drama teacher. Both were white-faced. They entered, first timidly, then, like the professionals they are, realizing how much their attitude would affect Alison, they strode in unhesitatingly. They sat with her for a while as I, not wanting to interfere in a part of Alison's life that is separate from me, strolled in the corridor outside. Periodically, I passed by the window separating Alison's room from the hallway, and I could see them laughing. Afterward Dom said, "We were afraid to come here, but Alison put us at ease. She made us feel good." She, in turn, told me with shining eyes that Mr. McLaughlin had promised she would still have one of the leading roles in next year's play. I think she is ready to go back to rehabilitation right now and start working toward the moment when she can be up on the stage again.

Saturday, August 3, 7:30 P.M.

Alison is depressed. She wants to go home.

Saturday, August 3, 9:30 P.M.

Each of the three other girls who shared Alison's room at one time or another during the past few days has left, all after stays of a few days or less. Alison says that is hardest to face. "I keep thinking I'll have to stay here for a few weeks, but then I'll be all right. They'll make me better and I'll go home and everything will be the way it was before. And then I remember. It won't."

I went home for a few hours today while Charly stayed with Alison. Strange to be at home; I wanted to be back in the hospital. I took the time to take Figaro, our oldest cat, to the vet. He has a thyroid condition, and we must keep him alive and well. I don't want anything more in Alison's life to change.

I brought Linda back with me when I returned this afternoon. I knew she would not be able to express herself; her thoughts and feelings are deeply hidden.

But Alison understands that too, and Linda's quiet, steady presence was enough to make Alison's day a happier one.

Sunday, August 4, 9:15 A.M.

Alison has a new kind of pain, a terrible one that I've read about in stories of people who have lost limbs in wartime. There's nothing heroic about phantom pain, which is not true pain but nevertheless hurts unbearably. Alison feels the lost leg and foot, which she says tingle as though they were asleep. "I wish I had a foot so I could stamp on it," she says. No medicine helps because, even though Alison feels it as surely as if the car were grinding into her, there are no nerves at the site of her pain, and there is no drug that can touch nonexistent nerves, tissue, and muscle.

In the last few days she's refused narcotics by trying to get by with less powerful painkillers. "I don't want to be out of it," she explained. I could see this was a relief to everyone: pediatric residents, nurses, and Alison. She's taking only Tylenol now but, although it helps her to relax, it doesn't help to alleviate the pain.

Distraction helps. So at 6:15 A.M. I bathed Alison, long before the other patients were up. Actually, she does most of it herself, being able now to sit propped upright in the bed for short periods, long enough for her morning sponge bath. By the time Dr. Livingston comes in at 7:30 or so, Alison is dressed in a fresh nightgown, her own now, a change from the hospital gowns she wore for almost a week because they were easier to put on and take off. Dr. Livingston notices each new gown. And she has new ones. I made sure of that when I went home on Saturday morning.

Yesterday afternoon she said, "I have to wash my hair." Ten days of not washing her hair, for a girl who ordinarily washes it every day, ten days of lying in a hospital bed with the grime of that Tenafly street still matting her hair, had become too much for her to tolerate, even at the cost of the discomfort that we both knew shampooing would entail. "I have to wash my hair," she said. It was as though she said, "I'm going to be fine."

One of the nurses' aides, a kind woman who had cared for Alison in intensive care, said she would shampoo Alison's hair today by putting her on a stretcher, wheeling her to the high sink on the other side of the room, and hanging her head over the edge of the stretcher. But the aide is off duty today, and I wouldn't approach any of the others. Nor can I imagine shifting Alison around that much. So we devised our own system at seven this morning. Carefully and slowly I maneuvered her so that she lay across the bed with her head over the edge. I placed a basin on a chair, and it worked! The head nurse would say it was against the rules, probably rule number 4,623, but it's done and Alison is happy about it.

For the past several evenings and this whole weekend, kids from school have visited. Some are not even her friends, just acquaintances from chorus or shared classes. But they care about her and show it. Though they have done most of the talking, Alison likes them and their stories. Today was different, though. Alison felt pretty again, and she joined in the conversation, sitting up in bed in a new nightshirt that looks like nothing more than an elongated T-shirt, but is the one she likes best, and with clean, fluffy hair once more. The stump is covered by the sheet, the top of her is unchanged, and she is surrounded by young people.

Six

FRIENDS

Monday, August 5, 7:30 A.M.

Alison is leaping ahead in her recovery. She's wearing me out with her energy and her will to move forward; I love it.

She still has a lot of phantom pain. Yesterday, in the late morning, it was terrible, and I couldn't leave her for a moment. The nurses are loath to give narcotics, though Alison is now asking for them again. Tylenol with codeine does seem to help a little, if only in the mind. All of the doctors are concerned and unwilling to leave her in pain.

But in the afternoon, with nonstop company and later with Peter here, she livened. He has come down from Dartmouth every Sunday and Monday after acting in the Kurt Weill play the college is staging each Friday and Saturday night. It is interesting to see new visitors approach the room. They tiptoe down the hallway, then stop outside Alison's room, peering in timorously through the glass wall. I go out to meet them at the doorway and can feel their tension, their holding back, afraid of what they will see, of what they will have to say. Finally, they approach the bed, a wide, forced smile on their faces, their cheeks pale. Then they see Alison's welcoming look, her shining eyes that light up at seeing her friends, her happy greeting. They may see the outline of the stump under the light sheet cover if she is in bed, or if she is in the wheelchair they may see it in the elastic bandage. But after the initial look at the stump, the object of their fear, their eyes are drawn to her face, and the tension leaves their bodies. She is reaching out to them, to everyone who comes into the room. She is not allowing them to be embarrassed or afraid. She smiles, she laughs, yet she's realistic, talking to the other youngsters about her accident and about her injuries, and talking even of a changed future back in school.

She uses the trapeze often, determined to strengthen her arms and to get up onto crutches. With it, using a swinging motion, she can nearly maneuver herself into the wheelchair, another act toward independence.

Monday, August 5, 4:30 P.M.

Peter accompanied us to rehabilitation this morning. What we saw was poignant. Alison stood, weak and shaky, between parallel bars. It was the first time I saw her standing with one leg and a stump. The therapist started her out with her back to the mirrors at the rear of the room. When Alison's laborious little hops got her to the other end of the parallel bars, she was helped to turn and then she hopped back, now seeing herself in the mirror. What went through her mind?

Peter's thoughts were reflected in his sad expression. Yet, I felt exhilarated. Her will to walk leaves only admiration and awe.

Now Alison doesn't hesitate to hoist herself from bed to wheelchair with the stump, wrapped in its elastic bandage, in plain view of her visitors. It bodes well, I think, that she is at ease with herself and with others.

Sean Herbert, one of the twins who sent Alison the first flowers, has visited every day since last Friday. He's not an old friend; she met him just three months ago when she began working at Tammy Brook with him and his sister. Each evening after work he makes the arduous trip down here. Certainly he can't afford to go into a garage when he visits. Finding a parking space is not the least of the difficulties he encounters to be here each day. His presence is good for her. This youngster, eighteen years old, is a philosopher, a psychologist, a counselor, and a minister, rolled into one compact body with smiling eyes in a face that shows his Irish forebears. He brooks no fears from Alison; he allays her pain, though he obviously feels it with her; he urges her to eat patently inedible food, an act she didn't even perform at home when the food was edible; he encourages, compels, and loves. His twin, Nicole, and even his parents, who had only heard of Alison, now have become intricately involved in Alison's recovery.

Monday, August 5, 6:00 P.M.

Alison spoke with Jenni on the phone for nearly an hour this evening, from her wheelchair, which must be wheeled down the hundred-foot hallway to the nearest pay telephone. But wheelchair travel is no longer a hardship. Alison is able to maneuver herself now, though her arms tire from the effort. I stood nearby as she spoke to Jenni for the first time since July 25, both rejoicing that Jenni is out of the hospital and resting at home, that she has visitors day and night, and that her injuries will soon be healed completely. Alison spoke without apparent resentment or envy, though she tells me she wishes she were Jenni. So do I. Alison listened intently as Jenni reconstructed a little more of the accident.

"You took one step off the curb, just to go around the telephone pole. One foot was still on the curb, and you were looking down at your feet. I was looking at you, but I looked up in time to see the car coming," Jenni said.

"I wasn't going to cross the street the way the driver told the police he thought I was going to do?"

"No. Why would you want to cross the street? I was still on that side, going around the inside of the pole. We weren't going to walk on the other side of the street. We would have had to cross the street again to go home. That wouldn't have made sense. And there's no sidewalk on the other side either."

Alison sighed. "I'm glad. I can't remember anything. I wondered if I could have wanted to cross the street."

"No way. You never thought of crossing that street."

Alison's bouncy voice, the one I was accustomed to hearing when she spoke to friends on the phone, returned. "I'm anxious to get started on rehab and work really hard, so maybe it won't take so long and I can come home sooner."

She wants to do everything for herself. Now she combs her hair often, just as she has done since she entered her teens, and she can't wait to conquer the next hurdle.

Tuesday, August 6, 3:15 P.M.

The phantom pain is overpowering. Nothing can be done for it. To their credit, all the doctors are trying hard, but their efforts are frustratingly useless. Even Wayne Siegmann, who was here again today, said there was nothing to do for it and that it is likely to last for years. It has taken over Alison's entire life. Visitors help, especially the kids, but the pain is always there, etched on her face.

Tuesday, August 6, 7:00 P.M.

Dr. Livingston is anxious to get Alison out of Bellevue, though it's much sooner than the four weeks he originally predicted. There is so little she can do here, and the visiting privileges, though relaxed, are still constrained. He's tried to have her taken outdoors, but I'm not permitted to take her. Except for one outing, to a small area just off the street with cement benches and a few wispy trees that constitutes a park in this downtown New York neighborhood, she has not been out. She was depressed by the wheelchair trip outside anyway, so it's just as well that the volunteers are too busy to take her. There is a teenage playroom at the end of the hall near the telephone, but she doesn't like it, and I can't blame her. She can't speak to anyone there except the counselors because so few of the other youngsters speak English. The very small children are cute and distracting, but they have their own room for play.

This is a world that we would otherwise never see. There is a lanky wheelchair daredevil with a bullet hole in his side. There is another boy, age fifteen, who must spend his days on his stomach on a stretcher—with a knife wound in his back. We see them as I push the wheelchair around the hallway or as we travel to the telephone. We see the other patients, but Alison has met few of them, though the little ones come in frequently to see the flower garden (as do many adults who pass by and then stop in wonder at the flowers, end to end on the wide windowsill). Some of these children are here because of illness; many are here because they have been abused—eyes blackened, limbs broken. They like the flowers, but more than that, they crave love and attention. They would stay all day just because an adult is spending time with them. I can't give them much attention, not the kind they need, lasting attention and care. What little I can give is for short periods only, because the children become wearing for Alison. No one uses the word "abused." When asked, the nurses and the children give the same reason for the hospitalization: "He fell off the top of a bunkbed." It appears there are a lot of children sleeping in bunkbeds and falling out of them.

Across from the bank of telephones on the other

side of the eighth floor is a wooden statue of a woman. At the time it was carved it was surely meant to represent motherhood, a loving mom with her arms around her several children. It's moving and evocative of what a mother's love should be. But many of these children are wards of the state, kept here long after they have recovered from their diseases or their wounds because there is no foster home available for them when they are ready to be discharged. Bellevue is their home, the nurses are their mothers, the doctors their fathers, and Alison's flowers are their backyard.

Wednesday, August 7, 2:00 P.M.

Alison's latest gift is neither fuzzy nor soft, but it conveys a message. Our town librarian, a woman I've known all the years we've lived in Cresskill, a practical, no-nonsense woman I would not have thought of as given to metaphors, found for Alison a wooden seagull, white and life-size, that flaps its wings when a string beneath it is pulled. The moving wings give the image of flying free.

And who hung the soaring seagull? Dr. Livingston and his entourage, hopping from chair to chair to secure the bird high up on the ceiling, near the window where it can watch its brethren soar over the East River. As always, there was laughter, banter, and camaraderie. I love this man, a stranger, because of what he does for Alison. He bounces in each morning, expecting, willing Alison to be cheerful. Even if she isn't feeling happy, she brightens for him. I think much of her determination to recover and to live again is be-

cause of him and what he teaches her each morning.
He notices her hairdo, her fresh manicure, her varied
nightshirts. I think he rejoices in her strength as much
as I do.

The contrast between Dr. Livingston and the psychiatrist who visits Alison for a few minutes each day,
a service provided for trauma patients by Bellevue's
pediatric department, is striking. That doctor, a dole-
ful man with a beard that resembles Freud's, repeats
daily that Alison must go through a period of depression, she must cry, she must work back in memory to
the moment of impact. Even our rabbi has spent his
time trying to elicit tears from Alison.

The psychiatrist's colleague, a woman who saw Alison a few times last week, agrees, adding that Alison's
apparent cheerfulness and psychological recuperation
are a sham. She is unrealistic, this doctor says; her
room of balloons and flowers and bears is not her real
world, and she will have to face that real world alone.
I told her Alison had an enormous support system that
would remain loyal, but she discounted that. We'll see.
To me, Alison is making remarkable progress. Dr.
Livingston, who elicits cheerfulness from Alison,
thinks so too.

The many visitors are bad, too, the psychiatrist
said. Their being here doesn't allow Alison to think
things through; they are not the "real world." We'll
see how Alison progresses, but since I know her well
and the psychiatrist, with a total of perhaps fifty minutes of talking to her, not at all, I would bet on my
assumptions.

Alison has been depressed all along; I can see it in

her eyes when she's alone with me. She hasn't cried or screamed at her fate, but her unaccustomed quietness communicates what she's feeling. Yet I detect also a will to live as normal a life as she can. In this "unreal world" of friends and flowers and teddy bears I think she is finding a special place for herself, one new to her, different, but special.

I've twice had to wrestle with the stages of grief: denial, anger, depression, mourning, acceptance. Though this time it has been tempered by Alison's spared life, I've nevertheless had to face loss once again. For Alison, the amputation of her leg is no less a wrenching loss than the death of someone very dear to her would be. She, too, has to come to accept it. But I believe that her renewed interest in her friends, her clothes, and her future life is a positive factor in her rehabilitation. Yes, maybe she has to cry, to scream. But it was six months, six months after Andrew's death, before I could cry, so diligently had I repressed the tears during the twenty-one months of his illness. And it wasn't until the fifth anniversary of the day of his death, April 13, that I could awaken on that date and face the day. But I didn't vegetate in the interim. I rejoiced in daffodils and fresh snow; in a cat's soft purr and a dog's insistent paw; in my husband's glance across a child's head and my eldest son's understanding of the birds that he loved and studied with care in our garden and in the woods; in my little son's bright grin and constant mischief; and most of all, in my new little daughter. I became as I behaved: accepting, resilient, and, ultimately, contented. And what followed were the happiest years of my life. Every milestone was

73

highlighted, every small joy was a gift, every day was appreciated. I hope Alison can have this too.

Wednesday, August 7, 4:00 P.M.

I suspected that the head nurse would eventually exact revenge for Alison's visiting privileges. Being in charge, she has the last word. The flowers must go, she says, all but eight arrangements, and all within a day. There are almost fifty arrangements here, each one different. Charly can carry out only two at a time to the car long hospital hallways and three blocks away, and then to an empty house. The head nurse will not permit me to give them to the other children on the floor because that would be "too much trouble for the nurses." This dismays me more than anything else. The flowers represent Alison's recovery, the support she is getting. The nurse can ration visitors, ration flowers, but at least she can't ration the sun rising each morning over the East River, for a short time making the city a magical place. There is beauty in the world—the world outside, waiting for Alison. But the drab green hospital ward, the dreary hallway, the shopping bags containing my belongings shoved into a corner like a bag lady's, these are not a way to find order and loveliness.

Alison is sad, though not as sad as I am at the edict. My anger is disproportionate. Maybe my frustration at all that has happened in our lives is being thrust at the head nurse, who is probably only following someone else's orders. New flowers are delivered each day. Now we sigh when the florists make their daily deliveries.

We know we can't keep them. But the head nurse did come in after I had made an initial effort to send some arrangements home and expressed appreciation for my efforts and for the flowers' beauty.

Thursday, August 8, 9:00 A.M.

Two weeks. Pain is coloring every aspect of Alison's life. As she sleeps, the stump twitches. Pain is on her face when she awakens. She is unable to eat, think, talk, or laugh. "I can feel my foot," she says. "I can feel my leg. It hurts. It hurts." But she knows it's not there. Her face grows gray with the effort of fighting this torment.

At times, she's helped by cassette tapes of distracting sounds: the ocean, a meadow, rain. One of the intensive-care nurses, after observing Alison's pain one day, lent her a tape of her own. For the past few days, when friends ask what they can give her, I've suggested these tapes, and she now has several. For a short time she drifts toward peace as she listens to them through the earphones of her little tape deck, the first gift she received after the accident. Could the giver have known how much he would be helping her?

Thursday, August 8, 9:00 P.M.

Now we have to find a rehabilitation hospital for Alison. I have tried not to think of the necessity, but I know we can't postpone it. Like everything else, from the police-car ride to Englewood Hospital onward, it seems unreal, something I never imagined myself doing. Charly picked me up early, and we drove first to Kessler Institute for Rehabilitation. I thought, What are we doing here? as we approached the low, wide brick building, set among green hills in Essex County, New Jersey, and surrounded by grass and trees. Inside, everything was light and bright, the large windows letting in the late-summer sun. Kessler would keep Alison as an inpatient for only a short time, the administrator told us, and then she would be an outpatient. That is all Alison wants, to come home. We left satisfied with what we had seen and convinced it was right for her.

In the afternoon we walked the five blocks up First Avenue from Bellevue to Rusk Institute, which is affiliated with Bellevue. Just another large, dark, overcrowded hospital—no trees, no grass. But we knew its reputation as the best available. They would keep Alison as an inpatient for four weeks, no less, with weekends at home. Its program appears to be much more intensive. Alison would walk out after four weeks on what is called a permanent prosthesis, one that looks as much like her own leg as possible, and would probably be using a cane. At Kessler we were told she would start school on a temporary leg, simply a metal rod ending in a foot on which a shoe can be worn, and she would have to use crutches. Now we have to decide.

Friday, August 9, 11:00 A.M.

My early morning call to Charly was lengthened today by our tossing back and forth the merits of the two rehabilitation centers. We both knew Alison preferred

Kessler, based on what we had told her. We also knew she would not express her wishes, for fear of influencing us to make the wrong decision. Now we've decided on Kessler, though we recognize Rusk's excellence. But we want most of all to have Alison happy and in as normal an atmosphere as possible. Rusk's pediatric hallway where disabled and brain-damaged children in wheelchairs while away free time together for lack of any other place to go, is dark and depressing. Just being in a place where she can go outside, where she can see the sun brighten green leaves on trees, will fortify our mood, if not Alison's. And Kessler is considered one of the best. I'm sure she'll learn to walk again, wherever she goes.

The decision was made easier by my phone call to Dr. Sudesh Jain, who interviewed us at Kessler. Hearing from me that Alison couldn't contemplate going to school with a temporary prosthesis, she has agreed to get Alison onto a permanent prosthesis from the beginning.

The impact Alison's friends have on her is astounding. There are groups of youngsters here every evening and often in the afternoons, too. Some are those closest to her—Linda, whom Alison wanted most to see and who had some time alone with her last Saturday, Andrea, Audrey, Heather, and Erica, Heather's sister, and always Sean. These girls plus Sean and others, some of whom are hardly more than acquaintances, visit, care, and form a cheering squad. She needs this support. The shock that our temple friends and the people in Cresskill felt when they first heard of the accident is changing to admiration. Nothing that can be offered us is worse than pity, and there is no pity shown when the young people come to visit. There is amazement at Alison's doing what none of the rest of us can imagine ourselves doing in her circumstances: embracing life and starting over, just as good—no, better—than before. *L'chaim,* Alison. To life!

Sunday, August 11, 8:15 A.M.

The pain. "I can't stand the pain anymore, Mommy. Mommy, I want to die." This child who has not complained of anything before, and who surely has not called me Mommy in years, now lies writhing in pain. We've tried everything—relaxation tapes, massage, wrapping the elastic bandage differently. One drug works, and she takes it, but it is a morphine derivative, strong and addictive. She doesn't want it any more than we want her to take it. If at least this were over.

Still, when young people come, she perks up and talks of her future optimistically.

Though the relaxed visiting rules specify four people at a time, there are rarely only four visitors here. Downstairs, at the reception area, they know about Alison and remember her first night here. They know about the girl who had her leg amputated because a heedless driver smashed into her, and they call out to each other, "Lehmann? She has unlimited visitors," which, of course, isn't so. The youngsters pass through that barrier and into the crowded, balky elevators. When they get upstairs they confront the head nurse or one of her underlings, all of whom follow her orders. I can't blame the nurses. At times there are eight people in Alison's room, which is very large and usually hers alone, but the youngsters forget and talk and laugh loudly. We don't want to jeopardize whatever visiting privileges Alison has, but we're anxious to continue this therapy for her, which seems to be working so much better than the psychiatrists', and we want to enable the kids who have made the long trip down here to visit with Alison. For lack of any other way to handle it, and to avoid having youngsters wait downstairs in the main lobby for just a few minutes upstairs with Alison, we've sometimes wheeled Alison into the grimy waiting room. It seats no more than six but has embraced as many as a dozen teenagers, their very numbers elating Alison. The dingy room, angry nurses, silencing parents—none of it matters to her as long as her friends are with her. But even then, the pain is an ever-present specter at her side. It shows in her face and in her sudden silences.

Sunday, August 11, 8:00 P.M.

Our cantor, Shlomo Bar Nissim, and his wife, Barbara, returned today from a trip to Israel with their children. They came first to see Alison. They are bringing up four children, three by Barbara's first marriage, the two oldest, boys Alison's age and her good friends. Barbara has known Alison since nursery school, has directed her in our temple children's choir since Alison was six, and has taught her in religious school; she understands Alison well, and she loves her. As I walked Barbara back to their car, parked in front of the hospital, she marveled at Alison's courage and then offered what I suspect will be our best advice: "Now you have to keep telling her how wonderful she is."

Monday, August 12, 9:00 A.M.

"It feels as though crabs are biting my foot," Alison describes her torment. Sometimes the pain is excruciating; other times she is able to enjoy her visitors, as she did yesterday. Peter—a dream of a big brother— came yesterday and is here today. We played Trivial Pursuit, the four of us, with much laughing on our part and smiling on Alison's. She hasn't laughed since the accident, and her eyes deaden when she is without a distraction to mask her pain.

Monday, August 12, 2:00 P.M.

When the pain overrides all else, we put Alison in the wheelchair and wheel her around and around the great circle that comprises the eighth floor, pediatrics. Sean and Peter are wheeling her now. Frequently I do, sometimes late into the evening. How well we all know the bank of elevators, the double doorway to the intensive care unit, where the boy, so sweet, still totally paralyzed, looks into his overhead mirror to see who is approaching him. He is waiting for an infection to clear up so that he can be operated on and at least sit up in a wheelchair and begin rehabilitation. We peer into the premie room, with its population of tiny beings in incubators, each one just a handful. Then, the long hall of Eight West, where the under-fives are bedded in high-sided cribs, many of them crying constantly, some of them victims of their mothers' legacy of drug addiction, others whose only home has been Bellevue because no one else will give a home to a child with AIDS. Finally, we pass the room next to Alison's, where the children with psychiatric problems sleep, all in high-barred beds, accompanied always by a phalanx of adult caretakers, who sleep on cots near them at night and oversee them in a fenced outdoor playground during the day.

A month before Andrew died he was hospitalized for a few days for blood transfusions, a desperate last attempt to stem the inevitable after all the medicines had been tried and had failed. When he was most miserable, I walked him around the hallway of Babies Hospital, also propped up in a pillow-padded wheelchair to protect his aching body. As we walked one day, I saw another child about his age being wheeled by a seemingly impassive parent. Totally bald, making it impossible to tell whether it was a girl or a boy, this child was a youngster grown suddenly, hideously old. It was a skeleton, eyes staring from sockets set in a skull with skin stretched over it, above a body with no flesh left on it at all. Out of Andrew's hearing, I asked a nurse about the child, who it was, what was wrong. The answer shocked me more than the sight of the child. It was a little girl who had begun treatment for leukemia at about the same time as Andrew, a little girl who at the beginning of her illness had been a beautiful child with a mop of red hair. "Please, God," I prayed, "don't let Andrew die like that." That prayer was answered.

Tuesday, August 13, 6:15 A.M.

This has been the only day that dawn emerging over the East River has preceded Alison's awakening. Her stump isn't twitching. It does so, unmercifully, almost all day long and usually even as she sleeps. I would like to call it her leg, but I know it is a stump; I know that is the correct word for it, and I force myself to use the term. Strange, how much that stump has come to mean to me. It is part of her, and it represents her being alive.

Even Alison's and my acceptance of her stump was handled with the greatest sensitivity by Dr. Livingston. I remember when Alison said to me in a very small voice, "I saw my stump." That was all. But she began to accept it, just as I did. When I finally saw the wound, shocking in its rawness and the number of stitches needed to close it, with sutures thick enough to lace together a baseball and extending around three sides of the end of the stump, I cared only about the progress of its healing and not about its esthetics.

Alison's sleeping past sunrise reminds me again of Andrew, on his last day in the hospital, his last day alive. He had spent ten days there, battling infections, fever, internal bleeding, everything that besieges a person in the final days of leukemia. We knew it was the end. Just the day before the doctor had taken us, Charly and me, into a little room near Andrew's and had told us there was nothing more to be done, no more wonder drugs to be tried, no more hope for another week or month of remission. He allowed us to decide whether we wanted the blood transfusions to continue, his first act of compassion. We did not. Knowing what we were doing, we said no more, no more of anything. During that night, when Andrew woke up as he did each night, I must have been very deeply asleep. He called me. "Mommy." He never complained, never cried, never demanded anything. Just called, "Mommy." And I—how could I?—answered, "What do you want?" Struggling to wake up, to get up from my chair and touch him, go to him, I remember him asking, "What's the matter?" He sounded apologetic. He had woken me. He felt bad. They were the last words he spoke. I have never forgiven myself.

The next morning, for the first time, he slept past dawn, just as Alison is this morning. Usually, he woke up so early that the little red television set the people in Charly's office had bought for him had only soundless cartoons to offer. There was no all-night television in 1966, but soundless cartoons began at 5 A.M. He watched them, and everything else that followed, every day. How many episodes of "Superman," how many of "The Addams Family" did Charly and I watch with him? That morning, the last, he awakened late enough for talking cartoons to be on TV. But he was very sick, only half-conscious, and soon the nurses put him into a respirator tent. He couldn't speak. I couldn't touch him. All day I sat near his bed. I tried to read *I Never Promised You a Rose Garden,* but wasn't able to finish the book until six years later. All day I sat and thought about what I had said to Andrew in the middle of the night. But it was too late. He no longer heard me. I did not know then, and still do not know

now, how much he knew. He never asked me whether he was dying. I never told him. It was only shortly after his death that it became the procedure to tell children the truth about their conditions. We never talked about it. I couldn't even tell him how much I loved him that day lest I frighten him about his illness. I couldn't tell him enough how much I loved him that day. Not enough to last through his death and my lifetime.

Tuesday, August 13, 10:00 A.M.

Our last day together, Alison's and mine. I worry. She worries more. She will be alone for the first time since she lost her leg. Therapy will be difficult and painful and tiring. I won't be with her.

This morning, Alison's pain was such that she clutched the sheet on either side of her pillow with both hands and, groaning involuntarily, pulled on it with all her strength, much as a woman in labor might do. The head nurse happened to be in the room and was shocked by the extent of Alison's pain. As she spoke about wanting to ease Alison's pain, about Alison's having parents who care, unlike so many of the other children, as she spoke about her anger about these other children—defenseless, neglected, unwanted—the person whom I had thought of as the Wicked Witch of the North disappeared as surely as did the Wicked Witch of the West when Dorothy threw water at her. The head nurse has turned out to be the one nurse who cares most about Alison's pain. The others appear to be oblivious to it all, seemingly without ears, eyes, or hearts. The head nurse is concerned.

It's evident that Alison's pain is unusual; the head nurse says that in her thirty years in Bellevue pediatrics she has not seen a child with phantom pain such as this. She called the Veterans' Administration Hospital associated with Bellevue, she called a doctor from the rehabilitation hospital, anything to see whether others, who have had greater experience with amputations, could suggest anything. None could. I am now grateful to her. Flowers in the room are not as important as Alison's comfort, which the head nurse evidently cares about. Slowly, the little cap on her head has come to represent not only authority but professionalism as well.

Tuesday, August 13, 10:00 P.M.

We talked this evening about leaving each other, about our fears. Being with Alison these three weeks has given me strength to pass on to her. She said to me, "I can't go on. I can't. I can't. I'm not leaving here fixed up, the way a broken leg would have been. I can't do it." It's the first time she's said those words, the thoughts I feared she must be feeling. I searched for an answer. I hope it is the right one. I have no way of knowing what is ahead.

"You must go on. You have no choice," I said. But I believed what I was saying. "If you give up now, if you give in to this, then that driver will have won and you will have lost. It will be as if you had died in the accident, because if you give up, you might as well have died. You have to go on living, and living as fully as you can." I wondered if I could have summoned the strength to do what I was asking my daughter to do.

I'm frightened of Alison's coming back to Cresskill a different person from the one she was three weeks ago. The thought of her returning to school in the fall a disabled person, with a prosthesis, with crutches or canes, is hard. Will she retreat from people? Will she be afraid to reach out? Will she be afraid of others', especially boys', reactions? How will they react? How will she be changed? Will she still do well in school, or will all her energy go into her disability? Will she be willing to sing again? To act in the school play? How can I speak to her this way? How dare I give her advice when it is she who must face the world and the rest of her life?

I'm astonished to realize that I'll miss sleeping on the two chairs a few inches from Alison's bed. I have slept well many nights—not for long at any one time; the sleeping position necessitates waking up about once an hour and turning to the other side and the other arm rest. It's not comfortable, but I fall asleep immediately. How will I sleep in my own bed tomorrow night?

How will Alison sleep? How will she feel when I leave her tomorrow night? We may stay with her for the first day, but after that visiting hours at Kessler are 6:30 to 8:30 P.M. only. From being together every moment to not seeing each other all night and all day, how will we feel? But she has to regain her independence, once so precious to her and now again important, so that she can resume an active life. Since nursery school days she has been able to be on her own and function without me. Neither she nor I want her to regress to the age of three. But I'm grateful that I was able to be with her when she needed me most.

I took a walk early this afternoon. I wanted to walk back toward the East River Drive and find the emergency room entrance to Bellevue, to retrace the ambulance's path on that first day, to check what I was seeing in memory. I didn't have to see the emergency room again. That is etched in my mind. But the ambulance ride remains mostly a nightmare, and I still ache when I hear the wail of a siren outside. And so I walked toward the Drive and stood at the dead end of a street, on a ramp overlooking the entrance to the room where my prayers and hopes for Alison's leg ended. It was not unlike looking at an open coffin to be able to accept a death. This was the death of my child's limb.

Then I packed up my shopping bags of belongings for the last time and sent them home with Charly.

Wednesday, August 14, 8:30 A.M.

There have been good things about these three weeks: the closeness that Alison and I have developed, the strength she has shown, much of it demonstrated in rehabilitation on the sixth floor. She has gone to therapy each day, but after the first time I no longer accompanied her. This, like her relationships with her school and teachers, was her world.

But yesterday was "show and tell" day, and I was invited to watch her accomplishments. She uses the crutches carefully and slowly, as she has been taught, and is learning to compensate for the new distribution of weight. The therapist says she "transfers," jargon which means to move from standing to sitting, or into a car, exceptionally well. She can open doors while on crutches, even use the commode that they have set up in the physical therapy room for training. This is a new application of the agility and grace she has always shown, whether as a four-year-old in pre-ballet class or on the dance floor with her friends at her confirmation party.

And Bellevue itself has been good to us, most notably the ICU nurses, several of whom still stop by and visit. And the woman behind the counter at the cafeteria downstairs, who was always cheerful and who knew I wanted my breakfast of poached egg on toast fast so that I could get back to my patient, though she had no idea who that might be. And the people at the reception desk, who overlooked all hospital regulations and, to the horror of the ward nurses, let all visitors upstairs, thus hastening Alison's recovery. And the young medical students, the pediatric interns and residents, who became Alison's friends and who tried hard to keep her comfortable. There was the orthopedic team, who came in each day to check on the rod that is inserted in her buttock and extends down to the end of the stump. That team had its own share of zany young doctors who tossed stuffed animals around and talked to the bears, to Alison's delight. And Dr. Livingston's trauma team, its young students eager to learn from him but never too earnest to laugh with Alison. And, most of all, there is Dr. Livingston.

He came in to visit with the three of us last evening, not as a doctor but as a friend, and to say good-bye to Charly, he said. I told him again that he has led us all the way: telling Alison about the amputation even before the surgery; calculating the right time for her to see the stump bandaged, then unbandaged, so that today she is not squeamish or self-conscious about it; kidding with her, exhorting her to fight back, praising her good looks and her smile, brightening this room when he walked in twice a day followed by his retinue, dressed in baggy green operating room garb, but beautiful to me. He was there for us.

Dr. Livingston gave us his home address so that we could keep in touch, something, he says, he hasn't done before. He was evidently fond of Alison, who, he said, reminds him of his kid sister who is ten years older than Alison. "I'm reluctant to see you go," he said quietly, looking at Alison. "How can I let you leave? I'll miss you," he said, stroking her hair.

This morning he said good-bye to Alison, but quickly, and then he turned abruptly away from us both. I think his eyes were as full as mine, filled the same way as the nurses told me they were when he first checked Alison in the intensive care unit after the operation. It couldn't have been easy to remove the leg of a sixteen-going-on-seventeen-year-old girl who reminded him of his kid sister.

Seven

KESSLER

Wednesday, August 14, 10:00 P.M.

It was a perfect summer day for Alison to leave Bellevue and ride in the real world. She was wheeled
through Bellevue's front reception area, nearly all of
its orange, Naugahyde-covered seats occupied. Using
her crutches as she has been taught, she backed into
the rear seat of the car, but she was pale. Now she has
left the hospital, but not yet healed and not with two
legs, as she so often fantasized. Before, she had allowed herself to be deceived, but today she must know
it is to be forever.

I'm back in my own bed, as though I had never left
it. I left behind at Kessler a damaged and lonely girl.
I miss her; I even miss the indifferent nurses and my
"bag lady" existence, complete with cockroaches and
washing at a tiny sink with harsh, tan-colored paper
towels, just to be with Alison.

Not since she was a toddler in frilly pink dresses,
a baby I couldn't resist kissing each time I picked her
up, have I been so close to Alison. Now we have to

work at separating again. But tonight we were both crying and miserable, wanting to be back at Bellevue, together.

The people at Kessler seem kind and helpful. There are to be no more drugs for pain. Dr. Jain will be Alison's physiatrist, a specialist in physical therapy. She has had the stump wrapped differently, the elastic bandage wound on the diagonal, never straight across the stump. To avoid the need for medication, she'll use massage and an electronic device that gives off stimuli to deflect pain. The doctor who went over Alison's medical history with Charly and me called her loss "a tragedy," which at least indicated to us that the staff here, faced each day with amputated limbs and paralyzed bodies, haven't become inured to individual loss. The nurses have gone out of their way to assure Alison that she may call for anything, even to have a television station changed. With memories of uncertain responses from nurses and aides at Bellevue, she looked relieved. She won't be left helpless here.

She was put into a room with two beds, the other one occupied by a forty-year-old stroke victim. The first disappointment. Dr. Jain had assured us at our initial interview that Alison would be in a room with young women, and we had relayed that to Alison. I think she would have cried anyway, but on learning of the room arrangement she was even more dejected. Tomorrow they'll see what they can do about changing her room.

Gifts and cards continue to arrive each day. The dining room table was full when I came home. They only remind me now of Alison, so quiet in the back seat of the car as we drove out of New York through the Lincoln Tunnel into New Jersey on to West Orange and up Kessler's winding driveway. It's lovely there, but it's a place none of us should ever have had to see.

Thursday, August 15, 9:45 P.M.

It's been three weeks, and I returned to my office today, to the same kind of work at the same desk I deserted on July 25. But I'm not the same person. Empathizing with Alison, I'm an aberration in the normal world, the one where everyone has two legs. Three weeks ago, before midafternoon, my world was secure, as it had been since Alison's arrival turned what had been a house of death to one of birth.

On July 25, I thought of my golden-tanned girl in the sun, on the sand, swimming, but she wasn't doing that at all. She was being hit by a car. I have to think of the future, not the past. My head spins with all I have to do—letters, phone calls, work—and I can't focus on Alison. I'm sure that's better for both of us, but she has nothing else to focus on.

I've returned to work on a part-time basis. It was good to go back, and my colleagues' outpouring of concern is heartwarming. I can't talk to anyone for long, though. My time is limited; I exist only for 3:30 in the afternoon, when I can leave work, feed the animals at home (finally relieving Linda of the three-week chore), and then make the hour-long trip to Kessler. There I meet Charly, eat with him, and then arrive exactly at 6:30, when we're permitted to visit. The restaurant down the street from Kessler had many young, pretty women going in and out. I saw only the lower half of them. "They all have two legs," I mourned. Only Charly, ever pragmatic, and now impatient with my mood, forced me to marshal my strength in time to see Alison.

She needed all the strength I could give her. She has been moved into a room with three young women, but, except for going to meals in a wheelchair, she hasn't been out of bed all day. No physical therapy. No visitors, because they're not permitted during the day. She hasn't spoken to the other people in the room because they were all in therapy or out in the hall socializing. She's been alone all day, just one day removed from never being alone and from having the stimulation of daily physical therapy. I sought out the social worker assigned to Alison and inquired why this was being done. "It is necessary," she said, "so that Alison goes through a period of depression. She must be depressed. By being alone she is being forced to think." I know she is. But it's hard to accept.

Frustrated, I spoke to another social worker, a woman who lives in Cresskill, whose daughters know Alison from school, and who had heard beforehand that we were bringing Alison to Kessler. I had never met Carol Angarola. But from the time we arrived yesterday, she's been a warm and comforting presence, assuring us she'll help wherever she can and tending to Alison far beyond what would be expected. With Carol I finally sobbed, as I haven't since the first week during my morning phone calls to Charly. She couldn't disclaim what the other social worker had said, but she did promise to see that Alison is given some activity. She began as yet another stranger who was giving of herself to Alison, but in a short time she has become dear to us.

Alison had other visitors for a while this evening—Andrea and Eddie, Alison's first boyfriend and still a good friend. Their parents came too, but Alison was subdued, rousing herself only occasionally to smile or make conversation.

When we were again alone with Alison, we began to meet the other young women in her room. The room is a large octagon, with four beds placed so that they all face into the center, each one with a night-stand, a small bureau and closet area, and a television. Across from Alison is a twenty-eight-year-old woman who attempted to commit suicide by leaping from a fourth-story window. The gaunt young woman is par-alyzed, helpless in her high bed. Her elderly and un-comprehending parents hover around her, the father sitting near her, never taking his eyes off her, the mother puttering about to make her daughter com-fortable. On one side of Alison is a gentle nineteen-year-old girl with a perfect complexion and a serene expression. I wonder how much serenity lies behind the huge gray eyes and sensitive mouth. She was thrown from the back seat of a friend's car while on a visit in the Northwest. She's in a wheelchair, a quadri-plegic. There are many degrees of tragedy.

The bed on Alison's other side is occupied by a young woman who wheeled her chair to Alison's side. Nora Palmieri is twenty-seven, a victim of Guillain-Barré syndrome, which left her unable to walk. Three months of therapy have made it possible for her to take a few steps unaided. "Alison," she said, "I was just as miserable as you are when I came here. I didn't know anyone; I felt all alone. But there are great people here, and when you get to know them you'll feel different about being here." Though the twitch of her mouth revealed Alison's disbelief that Nora's experience would be hers as well, it would have been difficult to ignore the dark-eyed young woman's reaching out, her warmth.

Friday, August 16, 12:15 P.M.

Alison is coming home for the weekend! Kessler called to say she's able to move so easily with her crutches and is "transferring" so well that she can come home. They had told her and us that they never let anyone leave Kessler the first weekend. Nora also said a few weeks passed before she was permitted to go home. I'm happy for the first time in weeks. But Alison is terribly depressed, even with this news. She anticipates the weekend, but says, "I want to come home, but I want to come home normal. And I don't want to go back. I want to stay home, sleep at home, and come to Kessler only as an outpatient." Reality, not only that she has lost a leg but what life will be like without it, has crept inside her like a burrowing tick in an unwary host.

Alison called me this morning, restrained tears dulling her voice, to tell me about coming home, but also to tell me she was seen by a psychologist. She probably approached the woman with a predetermined idea that this person wasn't going to do her very much good anyway, at least after her experience at Bellevue and her lack of faith in the psychiatrists there. The psychologist's words went further, at least as I see it, than any others have yet to hurt Alison.

"Do you know any disabled people, Alison?" the psychologist asked.

"No."

"There's no one disabled at your school?"

"No."

"Well, there is now."

Alison was devastated. Although I pointed out to her that she hadn't thought of Wayne as disabled when the initial question was asked, that she doesn't consider him disabled and that she will feel the same way about herself, it made no difference. Despite Alison's growing realization of her disability, the psychologist's assessment pierced her like a bullet.

I called the psychologist to question the reasoning behind this dialogue. The answer I got was that it was to make Alison face her disability. Why was Alison being left alone in the room? I asked. Why wasn't she in physical therapy or occupational therapy or something to take her mind off herself? This was therapy, the doctor told me. She needs to be left alone to think and to come to grips with what has happened to her. And so she is forlorn and lonely. I can't accept it.

Friday, August 16, 10:00 P.M.

I spent the afternoon with Alison, learning to care for her at home. Her therapy at Kessler is the same as that at Bellevue, transfers with crutches, at least until a prosthesis is made for her. Her perky and charming therapist, April, instructed us. She showed Alison how to take a shower (sit on a heavy, plastic-covered chair and, eventually, have a special, hand-held shower head installed) and how to climb stairs on crutches. Alison learned and practiced to exhaustion as I sat and watched. And I learned how I am to change her dressing. I struggled to remember all that April was telling me. Each time the dressing is changed, twice a day, the wound must be cleaned with hydrogen peroxide, then with a special iodine tincture, after which several four-by-four gauze pads are applied to cover the wound. Over this is slipped a silken sheath, which covers the stump and the bandages, and finally the ace bandage is wrapped, beginning with several turns around the waist and then down the hip and around the stump. I must always be certain to retain the diagonal pattern. Over all this, another sheath, a netted one, is pulled over the stump to keep the elastic bandage from slipping around. I can write, I can edit, I can sew, I can cook, I can garden, I can knit, I can nurture. To a greater or lesser degree I'm good at all of these. I'm a terrible nurse. I hope I can do it.

Alison still has pain, but she's off all pain medication. Her increased activity today and the new way of wrapping the stump are making the pain bearable. Relaxation tape recordings, which put her into a trancelike state as she tries to fight her way out of the pain, are there when she needs them.

Sean and Nicole visited her this evening, and she was more responsive than last night. They talked to her about the importance of sticking it out as an inpatient, something she doesn't want to do, to get the most out of physical therapy in the shortest possible time.

Nora, in the bed beside Alison, is telling her the same thing, that a few weeks as an inpatient will affect a lifetime of walking. Alison is lonely, but Nora, everyone's friend, assures her that will pass.

Saturday, August 17, 3:00 P.M.

Alison is home, in our family room on the fawn-colored sofa, the leg support raised on the recliner seat to make her comfortable, the sun coming in through the skylight and windows. She's surrounded by her friends, which is all she wants.

She was as quiet on the ride home as she was on the one to Kessler three days ago. She shrank into a corner of the car. We picked up Thimble, our curly-haired tan cockapoo, from the dog groomer, and it was only the dog's delight at seeing Alison that roused any response from our unhappy girl—that and the soft-rock music playing on the car radio. Charly, who knows the notes of every Mahler symphony and who can listen for hours to Bach's Brandenburg concertos, for the first time in his life endured rock music in his car to try to break his daughter's misery.

As we turned up the steep hill just before our house, Alison sat forward. When the front yard came into view she set the dog aside, and her face brightened. Fluttering from the maple tree near the driveway were streamers. Balloons hung everywhere.

There were signs on the door, on the front patio, and, unbelievably, a six-foot brown-paper sign welcoming her hung across the front of the house at the second-story level. Linda and Jenni had been busy all morning. The big sign, the one twelve feet up, had been hung by Wayne, who had been watching the girls from across the street, as excited about Alison's homecoming as they were. Wayne, the man with one leg, the man Alison didn't consider when the psychologist at Kessler asked her if she knew anyone disabled. Just another nice guy living nearby.

Sunday, August 17, 8:00 P.M.

All afternoon there were youngsters here. Jenni and Linda have spent hours here. Jenni walks well, though she's still in a back brace and has nightmares. One of Alison's visitors was her good friend, Billy, a big, gentle football player who was confirmed in temple with Alison just two months before her accident. His letter from camp touched her more than any other. On two sides of the paper, in an agonized scrawl, he had written, "I love you, I love you, I love you . . . "

Despite some pain at times and despite bouts of quiet dejection, it was a good weekend. Alison spent an hour—a long time for a first outing—at Tammy Brook's pool, where her friends from work welcomed her. She went with wheelchair and crutches, her stump, as always, wrapped in an ace bandage, but visible for all to see—her badge of courage. She feels herself part of the Tammy Brook "family." And the temple family. And the Cresskill family. And our family.

But taking her back to Kessler this evening was difficult. She had done so well at home; it made no sense to her to go back, except as an outpatient. Getting into the car, she begged us not to take her back. Wayne was across the street and in our driveway as soon as Alison appeared outside, as he's been all weekend. Only he could console and persuade her. His mother, whom I haven't seen since the accident, came out with him and embraced me. "I know. I know. I still cry about Wayne," she said. As we talked, I mentioned Alison's stump. She looked shocked. "I still can't call it that," she confessed. "I never could. I call it his good leg and his bad leg." It doesn't matter what she calls it. She raised a compassionate, self-sufficient son.

Monday, August 19, 12:30 P.M.

Alison's morning phone call. They fitted her for the prosthesis. "Why? Why me?" The unanswerable question has finally been asked. "I want my leg back. I didn't do anything wrong," she cried.

Monday, August 19, 9:45 P.M.

The few hours we spent with Alison this evening were strange ones. Alison was euphoric. It started with Charly telling her he had seen a car bumper sticker in the parking lot that said, "I Brake for Kids." He wants to send it, he said, to the driver of the car, saying it was from Jenni Earabino and Alison Lehmann. Alison was so delighted with the idea of retribution that she called Jenni to share her father's idea. The quiet mood she had been in when we arrived disappeared.

By the time Sean and Heather arrived she was the irrepressible Alison we had known before July 25, shifting Sean around on her hydraulic bed and joking about the bizarre experience of being fitted for the prosthesis. She told them of the eventual possibility of her getting two different type feet for her prosthesis, to use with shoes of different heel heights, and of the need to use a wrench to change from one prosthetic foot to another. "Still," she said, "needing a wrench to tighten the foot is a lot better than having it so loose that I'd be in class swinging my leg and the foot would go flying across the room." She laughed at the idea and at her joke. The rest of us laughed too.

She enjoys telling the tall tale Dr. Livingston told me about the young man with an artificial leg who went swimming in the ocean. He took his prosthesis off under water and emerged holding it aloft and shouting "Jaws!"

A friend from another town, one Alison rarely sees, arrived with her parents in the midst of this laughter and silliness. They've been away for several weeks but came as soon as they returned home. Carrying a stable of stuffed animals accompanied by a heartening note from Alison's friend, they approached us with the solemn faces I had become accustomed to from first-time visitors at Bellevue. I'm certain they couldn't comprehend why we were frivolous at this tragic time, when they expected to find us wrapped in gloom. I suspect this will occur with anyone who enters the scene at this point, too late to have watched us steeped in horror, with Alison near death and in pain, and to have seen the depths of grief from which we've emerged.

Tuesday, August 20, 9:30 P.M.

Dr. Jain spoke with the three of us this afternoon. Despite Alison's hopes that she might leave Kessler within a few days, she accepted the doctor's judgment that the end of next week would be the earliest she can come home.

I watched Alison in physical therapy. She walks carefully on her crutches, putting her weight on her hands, not under her arms, just as she's supposed to, and remembering to set the heel of her foot down before her toe. There is no other foot. There is half a leg, wrapped in ace bandages. It hangs. It swings. It is difficult to watch. Yet, I praise her accomplishment, which is very real.

Afterward, Charly and I watched as the prosthetist fit on Alison the socket that had been cast on her stump. The molded-plastic socket encases her stump, from the bottom, where the knee would have been, to the socket's upper lip, on which her buttock rests. This, in turn, will be attached to the metal lower-leg section, and all will be covered with foam molded to match the contours of her own leg and encased in a stocking to simulate skin color. The prosthesis is large, more formidable than anything I might have imagined. This is now my child's leg. Charly and I watched carefully, asked many questions, and mourned. Alison was very quiet. That's her way of mourning.

She told me, "I haven't been without pain, except for one minute when I told you I had no pain, since the accident."

Wednesday, August 21, 10:15 P.M.

My mother came home from Switzerland tonight, knowing nothing of Alison's accident. I trembled as Charly and I waited for her plane to arrive. In the car on the way home Charly told her, again with his ability to recount Alison's loss and to say the word—"amputate." Twenty years ago, it was a long time before I could say or read the word "leukemia" without shuddering. Still, I can say "stump."

I'm grateful for Charly, having seen many fathers— more than mothers—break down when confronted by their children's tragedies. Many of the marriages of the people we met in the hospital when Andrew was undergoing treatment failed; many fathers couldn't cope. We knew of a father who, after his five-year-old daughter died, never again acknowledged that she had ever existed. That this kind of behavior is peculiar to fathers is only my theory, and whether it's because of their guilt for time not spent with the child, their inability to express deep emotion, or their reluctance to face reality, I don't know. Charly would have had reason to feel regret for the long hours he worked and was away from Andrew, but he was realistic from the first moments of diagnosis, both Andrew's and Alison's. The night we left Andrew in the hospital, having just learned he had leukemia, we came home after ten to a ringing telephone. It was a colleague of Charly's anxious to hear what the diagnosis was. "It's leukemia," said Charly, "and we're going to lose him." He spoke aloud what we both knew: there was no hope.

My mother has always been unable to show her feelings, be they love or anger, fear or loneliness. After the initial moment of denial in the car, however, there was no mistaking her wracking grief. "No, no, no. Not my little Alison," she sobbed. But true to her ever-present wish not ever to be a burden to me, she never questioned that we put off for so long telling her about our tragedy. She understood that there was no way we could have relayed it to her in Switzerland.

We had no worry about going to Kennedy Airport instead of to Alison this evening. She and some other patients went in one of Kessler's special vans to a Bruce Springsteen concert at the Giants Stadium in East Rutherford. It was her first rock concert, something she had wanted to do for so long. "I don't want to go with all those people in wheelchairs," she wailed, hoping we would agree with her. But we encouraged her to go, just as the recreational therapist did. Finally, because they were able to get an extra ticket so that Alison could bring a friend, she relented, and invited Sean. Sean is happy; he likes Springsteen. We're happy that Alison is willing to be seen in public, even "with all those people in wheelchairs."

I imagine Alison in front of me as I wake up early—

too early—every morning. But I never see her with her own leg anymore, just as, for years, I saw Andrew only as he was in the respirator tent on the last day, though I ached to remember back further to embrace in my mind the round-cheeked, cuddly, healthy little boy he had once been. This time I think it shows my healing is progressing, but it hurts.

Thursday, August 22, 11:30 A.M.

Alison called me at work, upset. Staccato words: "I want my leg back. I don't want to learn to walk like this. I want my own leg. It's forever. I can't believe it's forever. When I see people walking I get so upset. At the concert last night people were dancing, and I just sat. And I look so gross. At least people who are paralyzed still have their two legs. I'll never wear shorts or a bathing suit again. The leg is so gross. Why did Jenni not get hurt? Why me? Why couldn't I be hurt only like Jenni? She's fine. For me it's forever. I can't take it. I don't want to walk like this. I'd rather stay in a wheelchair." She had just completed another fitting of the prosthesis.

Dr. Jain maintains that Alison has to feel depressed and needs time alone. It's probably true because Alison said she didn't want to speak to or see anyone when I asked her whether I should call her psychologist or social worker. Carol Angarola is off today. She's the only one Alison would have spoken to now. She can't talk to the others—psychologist, social worker—she says.

Thursday, August 22, 3:15 P.M.

Her social worker came into her room, Alison just told me on the phone, and said she had something exciting for Alison. What was it? A handicapped sticker for the rear window of the car. Alison was appalled, not excited.

God, where are you? When Andrew was sick I dared not pray for his recovery, only for an easy death and strength for him. Both those prayers were answered to a degree, because they were possibilities. Is that the way to pray? In the ambulance coming down the East River Drive I prayed silently: "Please, God, please, God, please, please, God . . . " for Alison's leg. That's gone. What do I pray for now? Only strength, for her. God, I'm praying. Do you hear me?

I don't want people at work to know I've been crying, so I wipe my eyes quickly. I've always been able to cry so it doesn't show afterward.

I'm not sure Alison has to go through all this depression to effect recovery, as the people at Kessler and the rabbi say she does. Isn't it possible to come to grips with reality little by little without being plunged into an abyss, sometimes even by artificial means, as the Kessler professionals are doing by their bluntness?

Saturday, August 24, 8:00 P.M.

Last weekend we brought Alison home in a wheelchair. This weekend we haven't taken the wheelchair out of the car. She does everything on crutches, even opening doors, turning on lights—*and* turning them off again. She never did that before the accident!

Sunday, August 25, 4:30 P.M.

The grandmothers visit Alison each weekend. Charly's mother had been with Alison at Bellevue every Saturday. She repeats again and again, to us, to Alison, for whom it's oppressive, "She could have been dead. She could have been dead. . . . " Now we have to try to persuade her that Alison's life has been spared, and we have to go on from here to rejoice in this next phase: her recovery.

My mother, who saw Alison at Kessler the night after she arrived from Europe, was cheered to see her granddaughter, coping and resilient, and she has picked up our hopeful attitude. I think the dispiriting times for Alison occur when she's lonely, left by herself in her bed with nothing to occupy her time; when remarks are made purposely to "depress" her; when she compares herself to a group of teenagers, such as those at the Springsteen concert; when she's fitted for the prosthesis, feels this thing made of metal, plastic, and foam rubber on her left leg and sees it as her means of locomotion for the rest of her life. To me, these are real reasons to be dejected. But when she's with us or with her friends she responds to our feelings, and her spirit and optimism rebound.

Many of Alison's teachers have seen her. Her favorite elementary-school teacher was among the first of her visitors at Bellevue, but Joe Miller didn't see the new Alison then; she was still a wan little girl lying very still in her hospital bed. Two physical education teachers made the trip to Kessler one evening; their natural cheerleading style was right for Alison. Her French teacher made a needlepoint black cat for her—to join the three furry ones we have in the house. Math teacher, English teacher, school secretary—all have visited. A short while ago, Alison was sitting in a circle of youngsters from school, a small table in the middle filled with soda, candy, and chips. As I ushered the school's principal and vice-principal to join them, a hush fell on the group, but within minutes they were all talking and laughing again. The kids were impressed by Alison's visitors; Alison was pleased.

Adults still approach with trepidation. The kids bounce right in. The word has gone out: it's okay to visit Alison.

Monday, August 26, 10:00 P.M.

Charly and I are tired, so tired. We snipe at each other, and I am sorry because we need each other. We want to be close and we know the only way we can cope is together, but frustration and exhaustion interfere. We leave Kessler by 8:30, after a voice over the loudspeaker decrees the end of visiting hours. Driving my own car home, I must follow directly behind Charly's so that I need focus only on his rear red lights ahead of me on the Turnpike to get myself home.

We've engaged an attorney, but everyone agrees the driver, from whom we have never heard a word, will surely walk away from this accident. But the fund begun by Tammy Brook grows each day, indicating to us how many hundreds of people have been touched by Alison's story and want to help in some way. Once the management of the country club put a notice into the local newspaper the donors came not only from the club's membership, but from people in Cresskill and all the surrounding towns as well. This money will have been given from the heart, not because of a court decree.

Alison has put away the wheelchair, maneuvering only on crutches down the halls and in the courtyard at Kessler. She told us this evening that she saw a woman wearing a prosthesis similar to the one she will have. "I couldn't tell it was an artificial leg," she bubbled.

She's proud of her accomplishment with the crutches. Not as proud as we are. No, we are more than proud; we are gratified that this protected little girl with a carefree childhood—a life lived in a house with a garden to play in and a room of her own, in a town where she could ride her bicycle and run track, play softball and tennis, a life that always included parents who cherished her—is coping as she is. Two big brothers loved her: Jonathan, who called her "Big Al," even when she was two-and-a-half feet tall, and Peter, always patient and available. She's confronting a challenge beyond most people's nightmares, and without prior toughening.

My goal has been to create good memories for my children. Some memories have been taken out of my hands, though Jonathan and Charly and I now treasure what we remember of the years with Andrew. My

goal did allow Alison sixteen years of a charmed life.
Charly and I can remember Alison in school plays and
concerts, when we marveled that this endearing little
girl was our daughter; on trips, tied in with school
projects or the Brownies, to the Museum of Natural
History and to the Bronx Zoo, where each year she
tried to spy the newborn baby animals early in the
spring. At Broadway shows, dinners out, and on hikes
in the woods, which she shared with her brothers,
when, despite disparate ages, we could all enjoy each
other's laughter. Birthday parties. Vacations. Disney-
land, where, three years old and frightened, she rode
through the Pirates of the Caribbean exhibit with her
hands over her ears and my hands over her eyes; Disney World, where four years later she couldn't see and
hear enough; Israel, where we toured with Peter and
where she decided to change her Hebrew name, given
at birth, from Abishag, which a former rabbi had suggested to retain the "A" for Andrew, to Aviva, because
to Alison's consternation our tour guide informed her
that Abishag had been a whore in King David's time;
Cape Cod, where her favorite excursion was to savor
the kitsch and glitter of Provincetown in the evening;
Paris, where we met Peter after he spent a college
semester in Germany, and where Alison became more
adept at traveling on the Métro than at practicing her
fledgling French. And memories of the everyday, the
family days, when no special events occurred, but the
days passed by in peaceful procession.

Alison's bat mitzvah, which coincided with my two-
year tenure as the synagogue's first woman president
climaxed her little-girl years. She endeared herself to

her brothers and us, not only because of the way she led the congregation in certain prayer sections of the service and chanted from the Torah, but also because she had so closely observed my presentation of temple gifts to other children at their ceremonies each sabbath morning that she took over my role as well as her own, imitating my style and in effect playing both giver and recipient of the gifts. It's the only time I've seen a congregation applaud, and I found myself looking nervously at the rabbi for his reaction, but he was laughing too.

Tuesday, August 27, 11:30 A.M.

"I walked!" Alison exulted. During the fitting of the unfinished prosthesis this morning, she walked between parallel bars for fifteen minutes (though she'd been told she probably could stand on the leg for only a few minutes). I thought she'd be dejected the first time she stood on it because of what it represented and because she wouldn't be able to stand long. But she wasn't—she walked with it. After she hung up the phone I burst into tears, this time of joy and pride, as I telephoned Charly to tell him of her achievement.

Tuesday, August 27, 9:30 P.M.

It was a mistake to take Alison's friend Andrea with me to visit her tonight. Charly and I had dinner with the wrong girl; we walked behind the wrong girl with two legs and short shorts, white socks, and sneakers; and I took the wrong girl home.

Alison must have felt it too. This morning's exuberance vanished. She cried when I left. Sending Andi into the hall, I tried to comfort Alison, but couldn't argue with her words: "It's not fair. It's not fair. This is the worst summer of my life. It isn't my own leg. I want my own leg back. It's so hard, so hard. It's so forever."

"It's better," she said, when I compared her own mourning to our mourning for Andrew, "to miss someone who's dead. At least he doesn't feel anything anymore."

Wednesday, August 28, 10:00 P.M.

Nora's promises have materialized. Alison feels comfortable and among friends at Kessler. She greets everyone now, people of all ages, but especially a young man, paralyzed in a boating accident, who watches that she eats her meals and calls her the "flamingo kid" because she stands on one leg so gracefully. People like her and she responds.

Thursday, August 29, 7:45 A.M.

The nineteen-year-old girl in Alison's room has had a setback. She needs an operation repeated to re-fuse her broken vertebrae. She can't sit in a wheelchair anymore. I can see the dead look in her eyes, a giving up, that I saw in Alison's in the first weeks. I want to cry for this child who isn't my own. The daughter of a minister, she must surely have had many prayers said on her behalf.

Friday, August 30, 9:00 P.M.

How far we've come in five weeks and one day. Before I brought Alison home this afternoon for the Labor Day weekend, I watched her in physical therapy, taking one painstaking step at a time with crutches and the prosthesis. She rejoices. "I can look down and see two feet. I'm walking!" When I tried to imagine all this on the night of July 25, while she was in surgery, the vision was unbearable. Now it's something I've anticipated for five weeks and the prosthesis is welcome.

Alison has grown attached to Bob Silvestri, the prosthetist at Kessler, who put so much into making the artificial leg look as much like her remaining one as possible. His heart matches his talent. He knows what's important when you're sixteen years old.

Driving home, Alison was tired and closed her eyes. I recalled the rides home from Babies Hospital with Andrew after he received his weekly treatment. It took time for him to recover from the effects of hyperventilation, breathing so hard and so fast that he turned white and faint because he so feared the intravenous injections that kept him alive for eighteen of the twenty-one months of his illness. It was all so hopeless then, but I could never reveal that to him or to Jonathan.

Saturday, August 31, 3:00 P.M.

Alison finds it hard to wake up at home. She's used to hopping out of bed onto two feet. "I never will again," she said. Never. I was shocked to find myself surprised. I've been deluding myself too that someday everything will be all right again.

This is the first time Alison has had the prosthesis at home. This morning she wanted to try on all of her pants. I brought down the pink pants, the blue pants, the turquoise and polka dotted ones, and her jeans. I held them to me, remembering her in them when the school year ended in June. With Jenni and me tugging and pulling, an unanticipated dilemma unfolded. The first pair of pants didn't go on over the prosthesis. The lip at the top of the socket created an evident ridge at the seat of the pants. Alison shrieked. I stepped back, thinking it would be better if Jenni helped her try the next pair on. The same thing. Each pair of pants was too tight on the left leg, each pair brought more howls of sixteen-year-old anguish.

Besides the lip of the socket preventing the pants from fitting properly, the actual socket has had to be made large enough, larger than Alison's thigh on the right leg, to accommodate her stump, which hasn't yet lost its muscle tone and therefore its present girth, as we're told it will in a few months. The prosthesis is not a permanent one, one that will function by creating a vacuum between the stump and the plastic socket. That alone will hold it on. This one requires socklike sheaths to be pulled over the stump before it can be inserted into the socket. Additionally, a heavy leather belt encircles her waist and attaches to the socket, to further assure the prosthesis's function.

The mechanics of the prosthesis are unimportant to Alison. She's a teenage girl who loves nice clothes and wants to look like her friends. She's willing to be seen in her shorts and the bandaged stump. She was ready to wear her long pants over the prosthesis with her shoes on her own foot and the artificial foot. She wasn't prepared to have her pants twisted out of shape or jut out at the seat. "I can't go anyplace. I'll never go to school. I have no pants to wear. I don't care about anything." Despite Jenni's and my attempts to tell her the pants didn't look as bad as she envisioned them, despite Jenni's solicitude and willingness to do anything to help, Alison was inconsolable.

She wailed her way outside followed by a sorry train of distraught people: Jenni and me near tears ourselves, the visiting grandmothers wringing their hands but unable to understand Alison's anguish "after all she's already gone through," and Charly, the lone man, shouting his frustration at all this fuss about pants. Wayne heard us—how could he not?—and rushed across the street with the little hops he takes when he wants to run. Talking quietly to Alison alone, he was finally able to bring the pants back into perspective. I got into my car and drove to the best clothing store I knew so that I would find size-three pants with pleats, creating width at the thigh, and so that they would let me take them home for Alison to try on. I found them, French-made ones, and bought a pair in each color.

Alison says she'll wear them, grudgingly. She wants her nice, tight pants back, the ones like the other teenage girls wear. She's uninterested in the elegance, design, or sophistication of the French-cut ones. And, "I want my white pants back. And my yellow shirt. And my white shoes. I want my white pocketbook." She was wearing them the day of the accident. They're gone. The pocketbook was handed to me at Englewood Hospital. Charly took it home to try to clean it. I told him blood doesn't wash out. He had to find out for himself.

Saturday, August 31, 9:00 P.M.

Alison is in bed, the artificial leg leaning against her night table, her crutches beside her bed. When they first handed me the prosthesis to take home from Kessler yesterday, I was astounded by its size and weight in the oversized bag they gave me for transporting it. Taking it out at home I winced.

It was good that Alison depended on Jenni for help this morning. Jenni has been feeling guilty, her mother told me, about the discrepancy between her injuries and Alison's. It's not logical, but one that preys on her anyway. This morning she filled a need, Alison's and her own. Jenni still dreams of the car coming at her, still sees the driver's staring eyes through the windshield, and still thinks the driver might come back "to get me." She remembers everything. Alison's amnesia is sparing her that.

Alison had been harboring an equally illogical resentment of Jenni. Though I'd asked her to talk about it with Kessler's psychologist, she refused to see the woman again. I finally bypassed the professional yesterday evening and suggested to Alison that she consider whether she wasn't angry with the situation, rather than with Jenni. Alison became very quiet. Then she pulled herself up on her crutches to go to the phone to make Jenni feel better.

Sunday, September 1, 10:15 P.M.

Alison didn't wear the prosthesis again yesterday after the pants episode. But today has been a good day. The boys were home, ensuring everyone's happiness. This afternoon Alison wore the prosthesis to Tammy Brook with her shorts barely covering the lip of the socket. The mechanism for adjusting the prosthesis onto the stump, a valve two inches in diameter, mars the smoothness of the carefully crafted, nylon-covered artificial leg. She didn't care. She went, and she stayed for an hour, and she was among friends.

In the evening, we celebrated our thirty-third anniversary a few days early. Alison pulled herself up the five steps of our favorite Italian restaurant and then walked into the dining room in her new pleated pants, wearing her prosthesis and using a walker. It was good to have our family together. Overriding all other emotions, though, was our pride in Alison.

Monday, September 2, 1:00 P.M.

This morning catapulted me back to the terror of the first days. Alison has had headaches and an upset stomach for several weeks and is now taking an anti-ulcer medicine. This morning she woke at six, calling me from her phone beside her bed to my phone beside mine. She had thrown off all the bedclothes, complaining of being hot. She was soaked, though the morning was cool. She felt as if she were burning up; for the first time in thirty years, I couldn't find the thermometer. I opened her window, gave her water, made her comfortable, and went back to bed. But as I lay there a few minutes later, my breath stopped. Hot flashes and night sweats are a symptom of AIDS, which is transmittable through blood transfusions. Alison had six units of blood at Bellevue, Dr. Livingston told us, and at least that many at Englewood Hospital. I called Dr. Livingston. He wasn't in. I called our pediatrician. He wasn't in. In desperation, I called the Gay Men's Health Crisis Center in New York City, thinking they might tell me my fears were groundless. There would be no one there who could give me an answer until eleven o'clock. I finally called Englewood Hospital's emergency room. A nurse who remembered Alison and the accident took my fears seriously. She assured me that Englewood's blood had been screened since March and could be traced back to the donors. I called Bellevue and was assured of the same thing, though both hospitals warned me there was the possibility of her still contracting hepatitis from the transfusions. I can't worry about that too, so, exhorted by Charly, I relaxed. I'm sure everyone told me the truth about the blood screening, but the experience demonstrated to me how close I still am to panic.

By the time we had breakfast, at nine o'clock, Alison felt well again. All her symptoms had disappeared, and she came downstairs on her crutches as though nothing had happened. We probably will never know what was wrong.

Alison is in the garden with her friends. I can hear her repeating her story of the past weeks over and over, embellishing it now as her memory returns. She makes the experience of the fitting of the prosthesis into a comedy.

Tuesday, September 3, 6:30 A.M.

Today is the first day of school. Alison should be getting up, dressing in new clothes; I should be taking the annual "first day of school" picture, and she should be off, carefree and happy, starting her junior year.

Despite her inner turmoil, she accepts everything with dignity.

Certainly some of Alison's symptoms are from stress. She's had no more meetings with the psychologist at Kessler. I'm afraid she's putting on her "good attitude" for my sake so that I'm not hurt by her pain. I think she needs help, but I can't give it. She's right to shield me. I can't stand to see her hurting, and yet she's hurting badly.

Wednesday, September 4, 1:45 P.M.

Alison is coming home tomorrow. She'll go back only as an outpatient now. Tomorrow it's six weeks.

Eight

THE NEXT STEPS

Thursday, September 5, 4:15 P.M.

Unlike the brilliant sunlight that streams in each morning, the afternoon light filters through the oak and maple and sweetgum trees outside the den, allowing the room to remain cool despite the skylight and the big windows. This is Alison's room now—not to sleep in—she sleeps in her own room upstairs where the new stuffed animals remind her of how far she's come—but to live in, her living room. She is hostess, student, TV viewer here and, frequently, when I'm feeling solicitous, she is diner here. She leaves the room at night and to sit in the garden, and three times a week she will go back to Kessler for two hours of outpatient therapy.

She's staked out the corner of the sofa, the section that doubles as a recliner. Beside her are the telephone, the TV controls, her glass of fruit juice, and all three cats, splayed across those sections of the sofa she's not occupying. On the small, white rug nearby, both dogs attempt to curl up inconspicuously so that no one will remember to evict them from their woolly pallet. In front of Alison on the coffee table, an old wooden kitchen table with sawed-down legs and paint stripped to bare wood, her school books await the daily tutoring the school will provide. Her five subject teachers, a different one each day, will instruct her at home until she can return to school in a few weeks. We haven't been told how many weeks. A world has been built around a sixteen-year-old.

Friday, September 6, 9:45 P.M.

There is a strange sense of normalcy in the house: the telephone in constant use each late afternoon and evening, the TV turned to MTV, and Alison's makeup and brushes scattered around the bathroom—as before. It all feels eerie because I marvel at Alison's emotional strength. She's picking up her life, making it right for herself, even while she tells me she'll always have to use crutches when she doesn't have the prosthesis on. She gets up in the morning to feel just one foot, while she fights the phantom pain that intrudes. She makes statements without words. No more wheelchair, no more walker, no more need for crutches while she's wearing the prosthesis. Now she uses two canes. Don't help me. I can do it.

Tonight she's making the biggest statement since she hoisted herself from bed to wheelchair with her friends looking on. Tonight she's at a school dance. Not dancing. Just there.

Through the school, we've found a psychologist

who will be seeing Alison and whose philosophy mirrors ours. When I called her she assured me that she, like us, doesn't believe Alison has to submerge to the depths of despair before she can begin to clamber back up. Alison has cried some, but she has already grieved plenty. I think her instinctively optimistic nature is guiding her to trust that if she lives her life confidently, it will turn out well, but if she wallows, it will turn bitter.

Her teachers are amazed at her attitude. Her cheering section of friends is still applauding. I hope they'll stay loyal to her.

Saturday, September 7, 2:45 *P.M.*

Thirty-three years of marriage, satisfying, loving, good years, and some sad ones.

"This is the worst anniversary you've ever had," Alison said.

"No, baby, not the worst. You're alive."

Alison is working at Tammy Brook, checking in members at the pool. She's been there since 11:30 and doesn't want to come home until 4:00.

Her sense of humor, even when it is turned on herself, endures. At the dance last night a girl, inebriated when she came into the school, chirped to Alison, "How was your summer?"

"Fine," answered Alison. "I got around. I got to see Englewood Hospital and Bellevue Hospital and Kessler Institute."

Sunday, September 8, 2:00 P.M.

Alison registered for a postconfirmation class at a temple in another town last spring. Today she declared herself ready to attend the first session. As I watched her walk away from me, one swinging, slow step after another, leaning on her canes with Billy and Andi at either side of her, as I watched her walk into a room where she knew only a few people, the tears came. Of sorrow. Or pride. For what might have been.

Monday, September 9, 11:00 A.M.

Mornings are the worst. Alison wakes up with a headache, her stomach upset. As she shifted herself onto her shower chair this morning, she said, "I can't stand this anymore. I've had enough of it." But it's forever.

Monday, September 9, 6:15 P.M.

Following Alison's physical therapy session, we met with Dr. Jain. She's making excellent progress, the petite, sari-gowned doctor told us. Alison has moved ahead faster than most other young people she's known, she said, but too fast for her emotions to catch up. Even there, though, Dr. Jain admitted she is doing well. We know. We marvel. Though Alison hasn't expressed her attitude, I think it is, You can't look back; depression won't change what is, so let's get on with it. She doesn't need words. She's living it.

I'm writing thank-you letters, hundreds of them. In them I've written about Alison's spirit. I want others to know how strong and courageous this little girl is.

One person came to see how Alison is getting along. He's able now to go on living his own life and stop reliving a terrible memory. John Tessaro, who was at the scene of the accident, and his wife, visited Alison on Saturday. Dom Albanese had told us that the scene was etched in John's mind. As John was leaving, he looked relieved. "I know she's going to be all right," he said.

Tuesday, September 10, 4:00 P.M.

Andi's mother told me that Alison has taught the other youngsters how to deal with the disabled, but they've also learned how the disabled can cope. If they ever felt pity, they never displayed it in front of Alison. Rather, I detect envy in some of the girls for the attention Alison is receiving.

Alison will have a vacation, however, that might inspire envy in anyone. Her cousin Nancy, who is Jonathan's age, and Nancy's husband, Phil, have invited Alison to accompany them to Hawaii for a week next summer. Nancy and Phil love Alison as much as she loves them. I'm glad because I believe the anticipation will be good for her.

Soon after the accident Alison was saying "I'll never swim again. And I'll never, ever go to the beach again." Now, at Kessler, she's learned of a prosthesis that can be used for swimming, a lightweight plastic one that would hold her up against the waves. With it, she wouldn't have to appear with her stump exposed at a beach or pool. With that in mind, she's consider-

ing swimming again. Though I won't again see her
carefree pleasure at the pool, preparing to pass her
senior lifesaving test, I want to know she'll still be
there; she'll be different, more careful, more subdued,
but at least in the water and with her friends. Though
I won't again see her flying across the sand at the
beach, her laughter anticipating the icy water and engulfing waves, she'll be there. But she can't imagine
herself swimming with her friends again. Maybe the
trip to Hawaii will change this.

Her self-confidence about her stump goes back to
Dr. Livingston's lessons. Not only is she at ease when
she's not wearing the prosthesis, but she dons it easily
in front of an audience: Nancy and Phil, a friend of
mine, any of her friends who happen to be here.

And, maybe there *is* something to be envious of.
How many people, I asked Alison, ever have the
chance to demonstrate such courage and endurance?

Wednesday, September 11, 6:15 P.M.

Alison is driven to Kessler by a car service for the
disabled provided and paid for by New Jersey's no-
fault insurance laws. Under it, our own auto insurance
company, for the rest of Alison's life, covers all of her
medical bills connected with her trauma, including
therapy, transportation to and from therapy, the prostheses, and paraphernalia such as canes and crutches.
It helps us at a difficult time, but more important, it
gives us the feeling someone cares, whether by state
mandate or not. The company, through a rehabilitation nurse they assigned to us to act as liaison, has

been understanding of Alison's needs. They will pay for a swimming prosthesis in a few months, and they make every effort to time her transportation and therapy so that she returns by four o'clock, in time for the teachers who come each afternoon.

The insurance company doesn't pick up expenses such as new clothes for Alison, however: pants to clear the lip of the prosthetic socket; new long, fashionable shirts to wear outside the pants, to hide even the small ridge that remains. Nor will it pay for the car we intend to buy for Alison's birthday on January 31, the car Charly vowed the night of the accident he would give her as his gift of freedom. Never would she have gotten a car at seventeen. But then again, never would we have imagined her needing a car to provide freedom.

She has had several drivers from the transportation company. Today's driver told her he thought she suffered only from a broken leg, which was healing. "I was so happy," she said. "That's what I want people who don't know to think."

Alison and I sit outside each Monday, Wednesday, and Friday afternoon at one o'clock to wait for the van that will drive her to Kessler. She remembers how we used to wait for the day-camp bus on summer mornings when she was very small and how she loved to have me wait with her. I remember too.

Thursday, September 12, 10:00 P.M.

My days are full, though I'm working only part-time, during the hours Alison is away for physical therapy.

Though she tries to ask for nothing and attempts to do everything for herself, she needs care. Things have to be brought to her, carried for her, reached for her, at least as long as she is using canes or crutches. Once her hands are freed, she'll be able to be as independent as she's trying to be.

And, I have an added responsibility, a welcome one. Peter's two kittens, just three months old, are staying with us while he is away on an assignment for his new firm in Washington, D.C. They are adorable and loving; they are our entertainment.

Friday, September 13, 1:00 P.M.

Alison hurt herself in physical therapy Wednesday, probably on a treadmill that increases the speed of her pace. The doctor immediately took x rays, found nothing broken, and diagnosed a pulled muscle. She's probably pushing herself too hard, trying to move forward—literally—too fast, Dr. Jain says. But Alison is unhappy. "I'm going backwards," she said. It's not true, of course, but forward, for Alison, can't be fast enough.

Sunday, September 15, 10:30 P.M.

Charly and I have just returned from services, the eve of Rosh Hashanah, the Jewish new year. A new year. I'm experiencing again the disorientation of time passing that occurred during Andrew's illness and following his death. The time that has elapsed since July

25 seems like yesterday, yet like a year ago, a decade ago, a lifetime ago.

Many of the same people who had shown their concern for Alison earlier embraced us as we walked to our seats in the temple. I answered their inquiries about Alison with "She's fine," "She's amazing," "She's wonderful," and smiled. I knew, though, that Charly was upset I answered this way. "She's *not* all right," he says, glowering in his own pain. But as services began the quiet time suffused us, and my smile faded, my words receded. I couldn't look at the white-robed choir, where Alison should have been singing. Nor could I look at the rabbi, whose image I saw bending over the sad little rag doll of a girl in Bellevue's intensive care unit telling her to remember *shalom.*

As I do often, I thought back to Andrew, but Alison's face superimposed on his. I forced myself to think back beyond Andrew's last day, when all that was left of my nine-year-old was a staring wraith who barely knew me, to the days when I cuddled a smaller Andrew, one who was still chubby and healthy. But there are in my memory only bits and pieces of the child who existed before leukemia grasped him. That's all that's left.

My thoughts were fragmented until the *Avenu Malkenu,* the prayer that entreats: Inscribe us in the Book of Life. Each Rosh Hashanah this prayer is recited; each year we pray that we, and our loved ones, may be so blessed. Then the tears bathed my face, and my thoughts of Alison and Andrew melded.

Monday, September 16, 6:00 P.M.

Alison went to services with us this morning, climbing the long stairs to the sanctuary and maneuvering her way down the crowded aisle with her two canes. Billy met us outside, as though he had been waiting for us, and maybe he had. He sat beside her, deserting his parents, but it was plain that this was the way they wanted it. With all the people around demonstrating their joy at her being there, it was Billy's presence that made it possible for her to face the thousand people at the service.

All of us, Charly, Alison, and I found words and phrases with new meaning in the prayer book. I could sense Charly beside me, and Alison, on the other side of Billy, reacting to "God who made limbs . . ."

The rabbi's sermon was about hope. Maybe he should have talked about striving. Hope is passive, like my prayer in the ambulance for Alison's leg. When I lost that hope, if there hadn't been striving, there would have been nothing left.

We spent the afternoon with the Foxes, Heather and Erica's family. Alison enjoyed being with all of them, but it may have been a mistake. Sean and Erica have been going out since they met for the first time at Alison's bed in Bellevue. Alison has loved Sean as a friend, but at sixteen it's difficult for a girl to love as a friend a boy she's just met without having other emotions intrude. And they have. She is hurt, though she knows how much she means to Sean. Erica, Alison's friend since nursery school, has handled it with care, as has Sean. Neither one wants to hurt Alison.

Monday, September 16, 11:00 P.M.

Alison's sand-castle wall crumbled. For an hour this evening, she sobbed. She wailed. She grieved.

"I had the best year of my life before this happened. I should have been on the cross-country team. I'll miss marching band, and I would have been a platoon leader this year. My only goal left now is to walk in the school halls. I won't have the silly fun in college that I saw Peter and his friends having. I can't go to shopping malls. I can't go on hikes in the woods with Jon like we used to. I won't swim. I can't walk to and from school. I've looked forward to my junior and senior years—the best, everyone said—and look at me now. I was supposed to get a new bike for my sixteenth birthday; instead I got a wheelchair."

She and I were alone in the den. I didn't touch her; I didn't want to stop her. I didn't speak; there was nothing to say.

But she saw my tears and knew I understood. Afterward, when she went to bed, she was calm. Maybe the wall was not made of sand after all.

Tuesday, September 17, 8:00 P.M.

Charly stayed home today, the second day of Rosh Hashanah, and we drove Alison to Kessler for therapy. She's happy when I drive her instead of the transportation people; it became a holiday when we were both in the car with her.

She hasn't been back for therapy since last Wednesday when she pulled the muscle, and since then, until yesterday, she hadn't even worn the prosthesis. I can see, though, that six days is too long an interval between visits to Kessler. Even if she didn't need physical therapy, she would still need the psychological support of being with people who are not whole, who are not a threat, who are not Erica or Andi or Linda with two legs. Kessler is the world of the disabled, but the disabled who can and do accomplish. We made the right choice bringing her to Kessler. Its facilities and setting, the rapidity with which she became an outpatient and now the slow weaning away, which will continue even after she starts school, all are working, physically and emotionally. She's going to a psychologist at home, a substitute for the lack she found at Kessler, but Kessler's physical therapists are teaching her to walk well and carefully; that's enough.

While Alison was at physical therapy, Charly and I found a park and walked. Our walks, whether through woodlands, over miles of Manhattan's streets, or in our own neighborhood, have been an important part of our marriage. If we needed to talk, we talked; if we needed silence, we walked in silence.

But on this walk I was frustrated and angry. What we had to talk about could not be said, and silence was painful. Overwhelmed by fatigue and sorrow, we weren't able to salve each other's pain. The wooded path we walked, hilly and rocky, was something I feared Alison would never be able to do again. Only when we found a small town and meandered up one side of the flat main street and down the other could I accept myself on two legs without rage.

Wednesday, September 18, 10:00 A.M.

Peter's little black-and-white kitten, Hamlet, has been on my mind this morning. The kitten was sick when Peter took him back, and he's still not feeling well. I worried about him, and for three minutes I didn't think about Alison.

During Andrew's illness, he was always on my mind, even when I was occupied with someone or something else. When he died, his whole being filled me so that everything I touched and saw was imbued with him. Finally, one day some months later I realized several minutes had passed without my thinking of him. I didn't feel guilty, only relieved that I was going to go on living.

Thursday, September 19, 8:45 A.M.

Last night Alison called me into her room to tell me about a man at Kessler who had lost his leg, but below the knee. Only three days after getting his prosthesis, she said, he walked without a limp. First she related the story quietly, but soon bitter tears followed as she mourned not her leg, but her knee. "I'd walk like that. No one would see anything. There wouldn't be as much pain, there wouldn't be a limp, I could be in marching band in the spring." It's true. Above- and below-the-knee amputations are two entirely different operations, as we've discovered to our sorrow.

As I left the room, Zeke, a cat we adopted—together with her male name—on Cape Cod three years ago, leaped onto Alison's bed in all her rotund furriness. Alison's face softened and comfort flowed over her. She doesn't need teddy bears to hug when she's feeling sad. She has this warm, purring, special friend to curl up with, just as Andrew had his favorite, Mittens, who never failed to elicit a sigh of love from him, no matter how terrible his day was. Maybe there should be a pet for every sick and maimed child.

Friday, September 20, 11:15 P.M.

I dropped Alison off at a sweet-sixteen party this evening. "Don't help me," she said as she got out of the car. "I have to learn to do things for myself." She walked with her canes, so slowly, up the front walk, which was on an incline, always the most difficult for her to maneuver. The difference between what she is and what she was before July 25 is heartwrenching, but the difference between what she is and what she was on July 26 is beyond words.

Monday, September 23, 7:15 A.M.

Alison starts school today. She's upstairs, putting on the prosthesis. What a strange way for us to start the day! Only now do I understand what Wayne told Alison during his first visit to her in the hospital, that she will always have to allow herself fifteen extra minutes to get ready in the morning. When I dress the prosthesis as it lies across her bed in the morning, I feel as though I were dressing a giant Barbie-doll leg. It was hard slipping tiny clothes on those unyielding ladies; it's just as hard getting a pair of pants on this leg, especially as the foot remains in a flexed position. Each day I have to figure out which is the left leg of the pants to go onto the left-leg prosthesis.

I've been listening to the familiar sounds of Alison getting ready on a school-day morning: the shower, the radio tuned to her music, the hairdryer. But I hear other sounds now: the thump, thump of crutches, the clunk of the prosthesis being dragged off the bed and onto the floor in front of her so that she can pull it on. And as she approaches the red-carpeted stairs with her two canes, I hear, "Get out of the way, Heidi." "Move, Thimble." "Don't lie on the top step, Figgie." April, her therapist, wanted her to be able to deal with obstacles, but April couldn't have envisioned obstacles such as these.

Nine

CRESSKILL HIGH SCHOOL

Monday, September 23, 9:30 P.M.

All this school day I expected a phone call from a sobbing, exhausted girl. Even after I knew Alison had left school at two o'clock for her therapy at Kessler, I was afraid she might break down from weariness and dejection.

When the transportation van pulled into the driveway at five o'clock, it was the end of a day far longer than an ordinary school day. Alison got out, her words tumbling over each other as she described her experiences. There was so much to tell: the party her first-period French teacher prepared, with the school principals present, to welcome Alison back; her locker that was now beside Linda's, a thoughtful change made by Dom Albanese so that Linda could help Alison with her books; the school halls she shared with two boys on crutches while their broken legs healed, because the three of them were dismissed five minutes before the end of class; the kids and teachers who welcomed her without making a fuss over her; the ease she felt surrounded by people who have shown they care about her.

It was a good day. But her mind seesaws constantly. "It seemed as if the first day of school should have been the last, that summer is coming," she said. "I never had a summer."

Tuesday, September 24, 6:00 P.M.

"The last day of school" wasn't to be, and this morning began the second day. Alison, too, has to regain her sense of time, to recognize that two months have not disappeared from her life. Once on her way to school, though, her eagerness returned. I'm the one left behind, trying to catch up. I'm the one who watches as Alison walks away from me, as she did this morning when I drove her to school.

Yesterday, I entered the school with her, to return a film projector, and my last glance at her was over my shoulder at her departing back, surrounded by students and teachers. This morning I waited in the driver's seat as she laboriously left the car and leaned on her canes to forge her way to the school door. Linda walked ahead of her, carrying Alison's school bag—leaving Alison so alone. Because I'm careful to walk beside Alison, not in front of her, and I've seen Jenni do the same, I felt what must be Alison's pain. Such a small affront, surely done unthinkingly and without malice. But what a large affront to Alison's disability!

All around her, kids in jeans and skirts, sandals and

bare legs bounded toward the school. They greeted her warmly, but they strode by quickly, and I could see only their legs.

Yet, as she stepped into the doorway, a brass band blared, firecrackers exploded—in my head. This was a celebration, an achievement, a wonder. Alison was going to school! It's been just over eight weeks, just about the time Dr. Livingston expected she would come home from the rehabilitation hospital.

Wednesday, September 25, 9:00 P.M.

Two months.

Thursday, September 26, 8:15 A.M.

It was good to sit beside Alison in temple yesterday, Yom Kippur, talking with her, laughing with her (though we shouldn't), and thinking, It's not the leg that matters, it's that wonderful brain and spirit, which are still intact.

For the first time in twenty years, I didn't say *kaddish*, the mourners' prayer for the dead, at memorial services. I was rushing home, because Alison, whom I'd taken home at one o'clock to be driven to Kessler, hadn't returned yet. It was to be her first time entering the house without me there to open the door for her. She'd have to use her key and then ward off the dogs' delirium while still dependent on her two canes. When I called from the temple just before the recitation of the prayer to see that she had accomplished all this, and when there was no answer, my imagination churned. Choosing once again to incline toward the living, I raced home, afraid of what I'd find. As I drove up to the house, the transportation van pulled in. All was well; they had picked her up late.

Alison, of course, mocked my anxiety. Once again, I was *the* Jewish mother. My children tease me about my being "the ultimate Jewish mother." I don't mind; their teasing is tinged with love. I tell them they'll sit at *shiva,* the Jewish week of mourning, when I'm gone and laugh about me, and somewhere I'll laugh with them. Besides, I remind them, I'm not a Jewish mother in every way. They've never had curfews, nor needed them. A curfew wouldn't do much good anyway, they tell me, because I don't hear them when they come in. I'm asleep.

Friday, September 27, 3:00 P.M.

A hurricane was predicted for today, not much of one, as it turned out, but we're all home. I'm still writing thank-you letters, each one a description of Alison's progress. The fund initiated by Tammy Brook keeps growing. The club's members, strangers, contribute. People from far away. People in my office. Our friends. Our neighbors.

Alison showed me that she can dance. Seven-eighths of her is the same graceful, fluid girl I couldn't get enough of watching as she danced following her confirmation on May 25. Two months later . . . The left leg is immobile, a fulcrum. The rest of her body pivots around it, her movements easy and rhythmic. She is beautiful and happy. "I'll invite someone to my senior prom," she declared, "because no one would invite me because the whole evening is dancing." We'll see. That's more than a year away. Maybe someone can see past that one-eighth of her.

Friday, September 27, 11:00 P.M.

Alison made a momentous request this evening, and I made a momentous decision. She is sleeping at the Foxes tonight, as she has so often in the past. It was hard to see her go. I miss her when she's not near me, but that's why I agreed she should go.

Charly and I spent the evening together. "It's nice," he said. "Yes," I said, "but my mind is always on Alison."

As we watched the Boston Pops on TV, they played the march from *Star Wars,* and I remembered the school's marching band playing it when Alison was still a part of the saxophone section. As long as she has a prosthesis like this one, she can never be a part of the band again, because she can't lift her artificial knee even to simulate a marching step. And she'll have this prosthesis, one that can't use a more sophisticated hydraulic knee, unless she undergoes another operation to shorten the stump. As it is, we found out the first day she was in Kessler, the stump is too long to fit a hydraulic knee onto it. It's difficult to imagine a stump as too long, but I understand the concept of needing three inches above the artificial knee to fit it correctly. The operation would mean more anesthesia, more pain, more recuperation, probably more therapy, but she says she wants to have it done in a year or two. Too late, in any case, to march with the band next fall.

Itzhak Perlman played Bruch's First Violin Concerto, my favorite, on the TV program. One of the most moving moments I can remember was when Charly and I attended a benefit concert for the New York Philharmonic at Avery Fisher Hall some years ago. We sat in the mezzanine, and below us, about to make an unannounced appearance, came Itzhak Perlman down the aisle, the long aisle from the back of the concert hall to the stage, leaning heavily on his crutches, his thick black hair bobbing with each step. My admiration swelled, not only for his ability to make music that could invade one's soul, but for his attitude toward his disability, a result of childhood polio. I wonder how Itzhak Perlman's mother feels.

Saturday, September 28, 10:00 P.M.

Something happened today that I feel is important in the way we see Alison and the way she sees herself.

Alison was happy with Heather and Erica. Charly and I spent the morning at an outdoor antique show and picked up Alison in time for her to go to the football game. We drove her down to the school, intending to take her as far as the little bridge that crosses a stream just outside the football field area. At that point she would have about three hundred feet to walk, over gravel and grass, to reach the bleachers. She hasn't done anything like it before. But as we reached the front of the school, there were barriers up, restricting access to the roadway that leads to the bridge. A school custodian stood beside the barriers.

Charly said, "It's too long for you to walk down the road and then across the field to the bleachers. I'll tell him to take down the barriers." He sounded angry, as he often does when he feels wronged. But the custodian, innocent of recognizing Alison, waved us off.

Alison's anger matched Charly's. "Don't ask him for anything," she bristled. "I don't want any favors. I don't want to be disabled. I want to be normal. I can walk. Leave me alone." As she emerged from the car, the custodian, seeing who it was, quickly drew back the barriers, and we drove through after all.

I had sided with Alison, telling Charly he couldn't protect her against everything. But we were all wrong. Charly might have asked Alison gently, "Shall I ask him to move the barriers?" Alison might have been more willing to accept assistance, especially when the need was so clear. And I might have let Alison fight her own battles, even against her father's protectiveness.

As it turned out, she had a wonderful time at the game (Cresskill won) and wasn't embittered about not playing in the marching band. She did walk back on the roadway from the bleachers to the school afterward (she was right, she could do it), to call us for a ride. She was ecstatic; she had spent the afternoon in a normal way.

Monday, September 30, 6:00 P.M.

I'll have to become accustomed to working full-time again. I do now, three times a week, leaving at the end of the day in time for Alison's return from Kessler. The other two days I leave at 2:30 so that I can pick up Alison at school. The insurance company has offered us taxi service to take Alison home from school, but she won't hear of it. That would make her different from the other students. For the time being, this arrangement is working out. I wouldn't want Alison to come home to an empty house anyway, and she's still dependent on the two canes and on crutches after she removes the prosthesis at the end of the school day. And, I'm glad to be easing back into work. Soon, though, the textbook I'm working on, with its forty-nine components and ancillaries, is going to keep me far busier, and I won't have much choice but to be at work longer.

I think often of Alison's younger childhood and my work. I was home when she was home; yet, except during Andrew's illness, I've worked since Jonathan was four. Though much of my work as a reporter and feature writer for a weekly newspaper was done at home, I did have to go out some evenings, when Charly or, later, Jonathan was home. When Alison started nursery school, I began working in the newspaper office during the hours she was away. When she was seven I left for a part-time job with the publisher where I still am. For five years, as I do now, I managed to push full-time hours into a part-time job by coming in early and taking no lunch hours. Only last year did

I transfer to a job that required full-time hours. It was easy for me not to regret my decision to stay home with my children; I was married in the fifties when that was the expected procedure and my working at all was an aberration.

Not working longer hours limited the money I could earn, and in the early years Charly and I fretted over every dollar spent. We waited longer to buy new cars, wore less expensive clothes, and bought color televisions later than did our friends, but I wouldn't have relinquished the time I spent with my children. Only since Alison was born, when Charly left his job as controller for a chain of department stores to become a financial executive in industry, have we been able to afford the things we had to forgo earlier. But my working now has made it easier to put two sons through college and now to contemplate the purchase of a car for Alison. Charly has always encouraged me to work, even before other young mothers did, though in recent years our financial difficulties were over. He is happiest when he can do something for his children, to whom he has become closer with each passing year.

Our marriage is based on our friendship as well as our love, on shared interests and respect for our differences. We understand each other: I understand Charly's soft and loving core beneath his quick-tempered shell; he understands my sometimes overwhelming need for stability in love, a home, and my life. But the early years were a struggle, not only financially but emotionally as well. Our marriage almost didn't survive the first year, the one in an apartment in the Inwood section of New York City. Charly traveled several weeks out of each month while he worked for an accounting firm until he sat for the CPA exam. The separations were hard. Each time he returned it seemed as if we had to start getting to know each other all over again. After we acquired a kitten and decided the city was no place to raise a cat, we moved to Cresskill, to a year-old ranch house, typical of the 1950s and at the edge of a development of three hundred similar houses. A year and a half later we were able to use the second of the three bedrooms, a new yellow nursery, for Jonathan—Jonny. And then, ten and a half months later, Jonny had company in his room, his brother Andrew. The bedrooms were so near each other in the small house that in the mornings we could hear the two toddlers holding conversations from crib to crib. They appeared to know what they were talking about.

The third bedroom became Peter's six and a half years later, we doubled the size of our tiny kitchen so that we could seat five people for meals, and we had the basement finished so that the boys would have a room to play in. The house was comfortable, and we thought our family was complete.

But the difficulties in our marriage persisted. It wasn't easy for me to bring up the children alone. Charly worked until after midnight four nights a week and left again at seven the next morning. He worked Saturdays. Sundays he was so tired that he could get little pleasure from anything. The hours didn't change when Andrew got sick, but Charly's priorities did. We leaned on each other, though we had times during and after Andrew's illness when it was hard for us to reach each other, just as is happening now. We found that mourning is a process each of us had to work out alone. In the twenty-one months of his illness, though, we learned to mourn together, and for eighteen of those months Andrew was in remission and able to lead a nearly normal life. On Friday nights Charly and I had time to go to temple, which became even more important to us than it had been before. Though Charly worked on Saturdays we had time for friendships on Saturday nights, and on Sundays we made time for the children, for trips to the zoo or the 1964-65 World's Fair in New York, or for visits to Omi, Charly's mother, or Oma and Opa, my parents. Later, after Alison was born, Charly began to work normal hours, and evenings and weekends were free.

Now, thirty-one years later, we're still in the same house, but it has doubled in size. To allow Jonny and Peter each to have his own room and to have a bedroom for the baby we knew we wanted after Andrew died, we added a second floor to our house.

When Alison was born two years later, her nursery upstairs was ready for her. Peter had his own room, with an orange carpet the five-year-old had chosen himself, and Jon had his room, with shelves along one wall for his bird books and mementos. Charly and I finally had a bedroom that was large enough for us to walk past the dresser while the drawer was open. They had their bathroom; we had ours. The space felt luxurious.

Downstairs, we had a new, larger living room and, for the first time, an entrance hall. We had a new dining room that could accommodate sixteen for dinner. It was used often later, when we entertained during Charly's temple presidency from 1970 to 1972 and mine ten years later. Two years ago we made one more renovation. What had begun as Jon and Andrew's bedroom and had later become a small sitting room, has been doubled in size and is the den in which Alison is now comfortable. We bought all our furniture from antique or second-hand furniture shops. My favorite pieces are those I refinished myself and those that Charly found. We've reached our goal of a rocking chair in every room. Each piece has its own history— where we found it, how we found it, and how we refinished it. Now when we go to antique shops we look only for small items; we've run out of space.

Tuesday, October 1, 3:00 *P.M.*

Picking up Alison from school, I wait as she comes out late, even though she's dismissed five minutes early. First come hundreds of able-bodied, loping teenagers, boisterously loud and heedless of traffic. I sit and wait, afraid to look at what I'll see, the contrast between Alison and the others. After most of the horde has spilled out the door, Alison comes toward the entrance. I've had time to think while I wait; thinking takes me back and makes me sad. But seeing Alison through the glass doors heartens me. She's not sad; she's radiant. She's laughing. She looks over her shoulder at someone who probably wasn't a friend before, but is now. The royal-blue sweater she's wearing sets off her winsome face and dark hair. She's not feeling sorry for herself. Her sense of herself, her sense of self-worth, comes out with her.

Wednesday, October 2, 10:00 P.M.

Alison has graduated to one cane. Overjoyed at this new achievement, she kept the leg—we're calling it that now, it *is* a part of her—on for fourteen hours today, not removing it after her return from therapy. Small increments of progress. But big ones too. It's been just ten weeks.

Thursday, October 3, 7:00 P.M.

As has been true since the beginning, the goodness of people makes it easier for us. Alison's social studies teacher allowed her to take an oral test rather than the written one the rest of the class was taking. She was touched by his gesture, his rationalization that the other students had been in school for three weeks, whereas Alison had been there only a few days.

It poured today, the kind of rain that whips down in sheets, continues all day, and soaks the ground. This was the day the school had a fire drill, at the insistence of the fire chief. Alison can't be exempt from a fire drill so she, like the others, crossed over the saturated ground to reach a faraway tree where her class was to assemble. When the drill was over, the other kids raced back to the school building. Alison had to pick her way back, water streaming down her face and her hair hanging limp down her back. Only her friend Jill and one teacher stayed with her. The other kids and even her own teacher forgot about her (I am not disabled—she's accomplished what she set out to do). But Alison's description of the event was not a mournful recitation. Even hours later when she told the story she couldn't resist laughing. "It was so funny, Mom. And the best part was when we got to a telephone pole that was lying at the edge of the grass to show where the driveway begins. I couldn't lift my leg up over it." She got a boost over the pole from Jill and the teacher, and the teacher then held on to her until she was safely back in her classroom. "I don't have too much luck with telephone poles," Alison quipped to the class, deflecting what might have been a tense and guilty moment for the others.

She cares more about her looks now than ever before. She was never vain, nor did she spend a lot of time on makeup or attire. She still doesn't, but she's developed a new interest in clothes and in creating different outfits, shirts and pants—she can't imagine herself wearing a skirt. She received several pretty tops as gifts after the accident. At the time I wondered if she'd ever again care enough about herself to be interested in the thick blue sweater, the oversized knit shirt, or the blue-and-white, button-down shirt. My concern was groundless; she cares very much.

I wondered, too, whether her previously excellent schoolwork would deteriorate with all the other things that are on her mind. She's apparently not going to let that happen. She's done well on the quizzes she's had, and each evening she spends several hours on homework. Just a few weeks ago, she was still trying to plow her way through the required summer reading, *Wuthering Heights.* Through part of Bellevue's time, all of Kessler's, and the weeks following, she read the first two pages—over and over.

She's seen the psychologist a few times now, on Thursdays. Alison seems contented with her, riding home quietly with me after her visits, saying little. I hope it has become a vehicle for her to express the anger she can't help feeling—about her fate; the driver; the people who rarely, but thoughtlessly, hurt her.

Friday, October 4, 7:15 A.M.

Alison is wearing the sweatshirt, the one with the black lettering on gold, that each member of the track team received last year. I had put it away before she came home, seeking to spare her sorrow on seeing it, but she asked me for it. I'm sure she's making another statement. She can't run, knows it, but continues to give the message: I'm not disabled.

I wish that the psychologist who told her there is now a disabled person in Alison's school could see her.

Saturday, October 5, 10:00 A.M.

Saturdays are nice. Alison is assisting the teacher of a primary-grade class in temple for her postconfirmation course and will go to a football game this afternoon. Charly and I have time to be together, to run errands. Last night at services Alison was installed as secretary of the temple's youth group. We're approaching our natural lives again, and it's all because of Alison's resolution to get there as soon as possible.

She fell in the lobby of the temple just before services. I didn't see it because she had waved me on ahead so that she could spend time with her friends. "I didn't crash down or anything," she said. "I just sort of sank down, like in slow motion, because the knee gave way when I wasn't standing with both feet together. There was no one there to catch me." Instantly, of course, there were hands to help her up. I suppose it had to happen sometime. At least the first time was on a carpet surrounded by loving people who were as frightened and embarrassed for her as she was for herself.

Sunday, October 6, 11:00 A.M.

Alison went to the movies last night, with Erica and Heather, another first step out into the world. Several people we know saw her and called us, amazed at her progress.

Monday, October 7, 5:30 P.M.

Less than a week ago Alison was jubilant about walking with only one cane. Now she's beginning to walk without any canes. She's no longer like a priceless china cup, ready to shatter if handled wrong. Some of her gutsiness has returned and she's able to withstand some buffeting. The towels aren't hung up. One sock, the one she removes, is always turned inside out when it goes into the laundry. The lights are left on, the telephone is abused. I can scold again.

Thursday, October 10, 10:30 P.M.

Charly and I had to steel ourselves to attend Open School Night this evening; the contrast to past years hung heavy. It was Alison's example that enabled us to go. Certainly we could face this if Alison has braved the difference for more than two weeks. The teachers told us how wonderfully Alison is getting along. We knew that, but it was good to hear it from people in her other life. I said to one teacher that Alison is coping and then corrected myself; no, she is triumphing.

On Tuesday she spent all day in school, then finally kept the dentist's appointment she remembered two days after the accident, and then went on to a shopping mall with me to exchange a pair of pants. A shopping mall—which Dr. Jain and other people said she'd never enjoy again, at least not without the aid of a wheelchair. She walked through the parking lot, halfway through the mall, and back to the car. She was tired, her leg hurt, but she did it, eleven weeks after the accident. The wheelchair we rented at the insistence of Kessler's staff is a haven for spiders in the basement.

The prosthesis bothers her because, through all her activity, the stump has shrunk so fast that she needs a new socket, long before the doctor expected her to. Because this first socket doesn't work on a vacuum principle, as the one in a later prosthesis will, she must wear thin, woolen, sheathlike socks inside it to fill it. She started with two-ply "socks"; now she's using seventeen ply. There are days when the temperature still reaches eighty degrees. She is uncomfortable, and it hurts. Now she's seen the prosthetist and has been fitted for a new socket.

Friday, October 11, 9:15 P.M.

We've all been on edge. I snapped at both Charly and Alison this morning and then dropped Alison off at school, each of us annoyed with the other. I tried to think it through as I drove to work. Her quick flare-ups at me, I realized, are a natural and healthy need to become independent of me once again, emotionally and physically. At the same time, we haven't had much time together because her homework and her telephone visits with her friends take up all of her time after school and after therapy.

Finally, during the morning, I knew what I had to do. I left my office early, at 1:45, after working in overdrive to clear off the pile of papers on the "things to do" side of my desk. At 2:00 o'clock I was parked in front of the school as Alison emerged to leave for Kessler. She was delighted to see me instead of the transportation driver, proving right my instinct that she and I need more time together alone, even while she declares her independence. We talked, something we do best in the car. It's true that she needs to pull away from me, and I must pull away from her, must again become less involved in her life. I have loved our closeness, but she needs to live her life with her friends, as she wants to do.

I stayed a few minutes at Kessler; the transportation driver would pick her up two hours later. I watched her swim, the second time she has during therapy. Only last week did the thick scabs fall off the scar of the stump so that she was permitted to go into Kessler's pool. It was, as it always is, shocking to see her stump, though I see it every day when she gets ready in the morning or for bed at night. This time, though, it meant seeing her ease her way down the stairs, holding onto the railing, and into the water. Yet, when she swam, she swam with her old grace. As she moved away from me, she looked like an amphibious creature, an unfinished tadpole. Then she turned and I saw her face. Beautiful. Triumphant. And my mind left the stump and focused on the whole girl. My determination to match Alison's strength returned.

She's at a party tonight, the third sweet sixteen. I wonder if she would have been invited to them all if she hadn't been hurt—or hadn't shown her mettle. I know, though, hearing the kids talk, that they respond to her because they respect her, not because they pity her. She's accomplished that by her own reaction to herself and by her openness, her reaching out to others. "I won't come home early tonight," she told me, "because I don't get tired anymore."

Saturday, October 12, 5:00 P.M.

We've begun looking for a car for Alison, bringing her along so that she can be in on the excitement of choosing it. She won't need any special equipment, though we'll get automatic seat controls to make getting in and out of the car easier for her. "And no special license plate," she affirms. "I don't need it."

Wednesday, October 16, 6:45 A.M.

I heard geese flying south. Winter is coming; coats and boots for Alison, which are harder to maneuver. Once before, the geese's migration foreshadowed a dismal time. In 1966 I was apprehensive about snow on Andrew's grave. But then I had thought of my little boy underground in all sorts of weather. Not rational. Just thoughts. When snow finally did come, it was peaceful.

Alison is walking without a cane indoors. Tomorrow it is twelve weeks. She limps, exactly as Dr. Livingston and Dr. Jain had said she would, but far less than I had feared. By concentrating on not leaning to one side she's trying to correct the limp further.

She's so natural and wants so much to be given no special attention that it's possible sometimes to be with her and not remember. I suppose that's what eventually will happen to all of us. That is an attainable goal.

I can go for a time now, especially when I'm at work, without thinking of Alison. I work longer hours, too. Alison has begun taking a taxi home from school on Tuesdays and Thursdays, when she has no therapy. She comes into the house alone, calls her friends, and does her homework. Still, when she has a day off I'm glad I can stay home with her. Indeed, it's usually my supervisor who encourages me to spend the time with Alison. Yet another kindness, for which I'm grateful.

Thursday, October 17, 8:00 P.M.

There's still phantom pain, not as often, not as severe, but still a hovering presence.

Alison holds mental conversations with Gustavo, the man whose car hit her and whose silence has persisted to this day. "Do you know what you did to me? You are free. I am disabled. See that pole? That's what you pinned me to. You took my leg, but you walk free."

Friday, October 18, 6:45 A.M.

Mary, the daughter of Jenni's doctor, told Alison that her father was in the emergency room on July 25 and that he was shocked by what he saw. He had told her, Mary said, that he had never seen such a terribly crushed leg, and he knew Alison would lose it.

"How long did you think it would be before she walked?" Mary asked him.

"A year," he said.

"Daddy, she's in school, walking without a cane," Mary announced, and related the story to Alison.

Friday, October 18, 4:30 P.M.

The high school athletic boosters club wants to donate to Alison its half of the profit from the 50/50 collection its members conduct at each football game. People donate a dollar or so; the boosters club keeps half, and a winner, chosen by chance, gets the other half. She's touched, as we always are by such thoughtfulness. She won't even be there to hear the announcement; we're going to Washington to visit Peter this weekend.

Sunday, October 20, 10:00 P.M.

The weekend in Washington began unsuccessfully. Jonathan met us there, and it was good to be together, but the days were filled with tension on Charly's part and sadness on mine. Whether we affected Alison or whether she felt the same way, I don't know.

Jon hasn't been around Alison since she began to walk. He didn't realize what it means to walk in front of her, at times directly in her path and nearly tripping her. Peter was caught up in Jon's plans for bicycling, walking, hiking. They didn't realize how painful their conversation was for her; by the time I was able to interrupt them dejection had settled around her like fog.

Charly, overtired and fearful about this first trip with Alison, reacted as he does under such circumstances, by losing his temper over inconsequential matters. Though I find his reaction unreasonable and illogical, I understand it stems from his terrible frustration at not being able to make one of his children—in this case, Alison—happy. *I* know how much he loves all of us; but sometimes it is hard for Alison to discern it through his anger. In this case, the inconsequential matter was the difficulty of driving in Washington. Charly refused to let Peter drive, though Peter knows his way and would have navigated well. Everyone was on edge. I was unhappy. By the time we met friends for dinner on Saturday night, Alison's eyes, and mine, welled with tears. Her quiet told me how depressed she was. She barely watched the waiters dancing at the Greek restaurant, and their staccato movements exacerbated my own pain. The dance is very much like the hora, which Alison would have danced as a bride.

At Jon's insistence, we had gone to a park in the afternoon, to see white-water canoeing. Alison walked over gravel, grass, bumps for at least a quarter of a mile. I'm sure her exertions contributed to her later collapse. But she triumphed, making a journey we couldn't imagine her doing, for something in which she had no interest, just so that we might all be together as in the past. I pointed out to Jon and Peter how amazing this walk was for her and they acknowledged it. But without a sense of what had happened over the last twelve weeks, I don't think they understood. Charly did.

The night she spent with Peter and Jon, and Peter's kittens, cheered her. By the time we left early Sunday so that Alison could attend a regional marching-band festival in the evening with the school band, she was happy once again, maybe in anticipation of being with her friends.

We have soaring moments—Alison's triumphs— but heartache is never far away.

Ten

"TAKE THESE BROKEN WINGS . . ."

Monday, October 21, 7:00 P.M.

As we sat beside Alison in her bed the first day at Kessler, we believed she would need many months to learn to walk again. Now, just two months later, she's completed therapy. She'll get a new prosthesis in a few weeks, and Dr. Jain suggests she continue swimming at Kessler once a week. But she needs no more physical therapy.

Alison attended the band festival for North Jersey high schools last night. Seeing her limp, the ushers wouldn't allow her to climb to the top of the bleachers to sit with her school's cheerleaders. Her arguments were fruitless. The father of one of Cresskill's band members, who meant well but doesn't know Alison's spunk, threw himself into the altercation and shouted at her, "I won't permit you to climb to the top of those bleachers." Just as the band director was coming to her aid and the ushers were muttering about insurance and liability, Alison retorted to her self-appointed guardian, "I've had the worst experience of my life, and I'm getting through it. *You* are not helping." She climbed to the top of the bleachers.

Tuesday, October 22, 6:00 P.M.

Sean has pointed out to Alison that the words in the song, "Broken Wings," were meant for her: "Take these broken wings/And learn to fly again/Learn to live so free." I think of the white wooden seagull in her Bellevue room; she will fly; she is flying.

Friday, October 25, 7:00 A.M.

We've ordered a car for Alison. With Linda accompanying us, Alison chose the Pontiac Sunbird, a little red car. Our experience with the salesman, a self-absorbed know-it-all, will be the subject of jokes and the girls' mimicry for years to come. They do that well; a week together on Cape Cod a few years ago provided a storehouse of character impressions.

Now Alison has to get her learner's permit and learn to drive. If dreaming about it makes it so, she's driving already.

I made the mistake of saying to Alison that she was lucky to be getting a new car at seventeen. Aghast, she asked, "How can you call me lucky?"

Friday, October 25, 6:00 P.M.

I had to pick up Alison early from school; the leather belt that secures the prosthesis around her waist broke. As we drove to get it fixed, she told me someone in school had asked what was wrong. "Finally," she grinned, "I could say I have a broken leg."

Sunday, October 27, 4:00 P.M.

Sunday. The sky is endlessly blue; the leaves are not yet off the trees and have turned from bright autumn colors to duller brown and rust, though some of the maples are still green. It's warm. Charly and I went for a walk in this subdued beauty, but I was dispirited. Alison was inside, watching TV. Linda was with her, but the days of bicycling, playing tennis, and bouncing a beach ball in the backyard are over.

Depression is always a millimeter away from the smiling demeanor I present. The first month, after the initial shock came the gratitude that Alison was alive. That hasn't changed. And never will. But now we've reached a slowing down of her physical recovery, and despite the times when sorrow erodes my pride, I know there's another kind of recovery taking place, possibly the most important of all. Alison has reached the final plateau of grief: acceptance.

Tuesday, October 29, 9:00 P.M.

Peter has brought us the kittens. He's spending several months in Arizona on an assignment, and has asked us to board them—though Charly, Alison, and I wouldn't mind if they became permanent residents. Their antics delight us and are a wonderful distraction. Hamlet is a dignified little prince. Ophelia is a calico of soft shades of gray and beige; her greatest delight is to pounce on Hamlet and then dash off, daring him to pursue. Figaro, nearly fourteen and amiable, appears to enjoy their frolicking. Rumple, placid and forgiving, attempts to ignore the newcomers, a difficult task. Zeke, our most recent acquisition, should have been an "only" cat; she tolerates them to within two feet of her presence. The dogs prefer each other but periodically bolster their self-importance by chasing the kittens until the kittens seek cover in the basement through their escape hatch—a little hole Peter cut out for them at the bottom of the door.

I've loved all animals since childhood. Usually they were all I had. From my birthplace in Zurich, I was taken to London when I was four. From then until age seven, I have memories of my nanny; my father, whom I still loved at that time; occasional times with my mother; the large extended family of which I was everyone's spoiled baby; and the results of the German Blitz over London: the fires and sirens, the boarded up windows and the wartime sleeping arrangements on mattresses in the hallway, protected from shattering glass. As a Swiss citizen, my mother left London for New York with me in November 1940 under the sponsorship of the only person she knew in the United States, a second cousin who practiced medicine in upper Manhattan. My father, under the German quota, was unable to emigrate. I didn't know then, though I suspect my mother knew, that he was just as happy to stay behind; he had fallen in love with my nanny.

I missed him. I missed my pampered life. Within five months I contracted several illnesses, culminating in a three-week hospital stay with scarlet fever. My mother, who hadn't been able to take any money out of England with her and who was unwilling to ask anything of her cousin, worked long hours at little pay to support us. Finally, when her landlady was no longer willing to care for such a sickly child, my mother found a family in the country that would take me in on a boarding basis. I went with her on a long bus ride through New Jersey to Toms River in May 1941. She told me I'd come back to live with her in September. I stayed seven years.

It wasn't until I was nine or ten that I felt Toms River was my home and that the Ehrmanns were my family. "Aunt" Friedel, widowed only a month after her son, Charley, then a year old, was born headed a household consisting of the elderly sister and the aged mother of her late husband and her two stepsons, sixteen and eighteen. All but Charley, whom I loved instantly, had emigrated from Hitler's Germany a few years earlier. It was years later that I learned to appreciate the fortitude of this woman who single-handedly held her disparate family together and ran a chicken farm, never complaining about her fate. Only when I was fourteen, after I left Toms River to rejoin my mother, did I understand that Aunt Friedel, overworked and underloved, had been reluctant to demonstrate her affection for me when I was little for fear that she would replace my mother in my mind. Then I realized how overwhelming her obligations were and how much she *had* loved and influenced me.

But my memories of Toms River are happy ones. Yet, I never fully belonged there; I never fully belonged anywhere. The war years of listening to Gabriel Heater on the six o'clock radio news for word about the younger stepson's whereabouts on the front; the postwar years of innocence, the family on summer afternoons on the front porch drinking lemonade and watching the tail-finned cars go by; the yellow school bus stopping at the hip-roofed farmhouse on cold winter days; the tan hound and the pug-nosed pup and the dozens of cats that populated the farm at one time or another; the horses next door I rode while imagining myself as the heroine of *National Velvet;* the ill-tempered cow I wasn't allowed to approach and the fuzzy, silly baby chicks that soon grew up into senseless chickens; the books and the dolls that for years were my best friends; and the people—the ones who became my family—these were my world. They made my life.

By the time I moved back to New York, my father and mother were divorced; he had married my nanny in London and all but severed relations with me, for reasons I never understood. My mother had married her second cousin, the doctor. I'd seen my mother every two weeks during the years I was away from her. We alternated visits: she took the bus to Toms River once a month and I took it, frightened each time that I was on the wrong bus, to New York once a month—I was grown before I could get onto a bus without getting sick. But again I felt as if I were moving in with strangers. My mother made every effort to become reacquainted with me, and it didn't take long before we were good friends. My stepfather, who was acquiring his first child when she was fourteen and he fifty-seven, had a harder time understanding the vagaries of a confused teenage girl. But within a year he became dearer to me than anyone, except Charly and my children, ever would. Aunt Friedel taught me the ways of people; my new father taught me the ways of the world.

When I was ten, another young boarder, twelve-year-old Mary Lehmann, whose father had died suddenly just the day before and whose mother was unable to cope with the situation, came to live on the farm. Mary became my sister. We shared a room; she taught me dirty words and that girls get pregnant when they let boys touch their hands. I listened to her woes with boys and teased her about her skimpy Betty Grable look-alike hairdo. We fought and we loved. I sympathized with her sorrow at losing her father, whom she had loved, at being separated without warning from her mother and her nineteen-year-old brother, who was serving in the army. I met him once or twice when he visited her while on leave; he wanted nothing to do with the skinny, pesky little tag-along who tried to stay with her new friend. By the time Mary married an army buddy of her brother's and her brother saw me again, I was no longer a tag-along and he no longer considered me pesky. Mary became my sister-in-law as well as my sister.

Charly's early life was more secure than mine, though he, too, had come to the United States as a boy, from Nazi Germany in 1938, when he was thirteen. He quickly adjusted to his new life in Queens and had just begun college when he was drafted into the wartime army. A year later, he was called home on emergency leave when his father died, and after that his nineteen-year-old world collapsed. There was no home for him to return to after he was discharged; there was no father for him to follow into accounting as he had planned. His mother was living in a series of rooming houses, though the family had been comfortable while the father was alive and there had been money and handsome furnishings left after his death. Charly put himself through college on the G.I. Bill and then, as a member of the U.S. Army Reserve, was called back into service during the Korean conflict. That was when he met Mary's future husband and decided at her wedding that I had grown up enough to suit him.

We married and had four children: the first, whose sensitivity caused his heart-wrenching loneliness when he lost his brother and who henceforth took solace in rivers and mountains and deep woodlands; the second, whose cherubic face reflected the aura of pain and fear by the time he was eight; the third, whose endowment was an ability to make everyone love him and who became the nave of the family; and the fourth, whose childhood fearlessness was translated to courage when she most needed it.

Friday, November 1, 11:00 P.M.

Andrew would have been twenty-nine years old today.

I know none of our children ever forgets Andrew's birthday or the date of his death. Finally, Jonathan has a brother again, a different one, but one he loves too. After Andrew died, Jon was resentful of Peter. It was hard for him to accept that the brother he had been so devoted to was gone, while this mischievous three-year-old was left and was the only brother now. It was not until Peter was in his mid-teens, finally no longer mischievous, that Jon found in him another companion. Now Jon makes every effort to spend as much time as possible with Peter. He has introduced Peter to hiking, to rock climbing, and to white-water canoeing, all the time enjoying the company of this younger brother so unlike himself.

Slowly, the vision of the Alison of four months ago, her slender legs below the short blue shorts, is receding, is being replaced by admiration for this different, gallant Alison, this once again independent young woman who can do everything for herself.

She'll go to the psychologist once a month now. Just as she weaned herself from each of her medications, including the one for her distressed stomach after she came home, she's now weaned herself from the psychologist. She has certainly weaned herself away from me, but my tears in the temple this evening, after those for my dead child, were for Alison, grateful tears for what is, rather than bitter ones for what might have been. Acceptance. It doesn't seep into the mind and remain; it swings like a pendulum, in and out, until finally it comes to rest.

Tuesday, November 5, 9:15 P.M.

I went today to the surgeon who operated to biopsy a breast lump found last year. That was benign. Today he found another lump and it, too, will require a biopsy, on Friday. He believes it is again benign. I am telling myself it will be.

The kittens continue to charm us, even Charly, who rarely smiles these days and never relaxes. He, who was the first to have faith in Alison's strength and the first to achieve a sense of acceptance of what happened, is suffering now from delayed grief.

I miss Alison when I'm not with her. Maybe that's part of what's bothering Charly. He's feeling excluded, though Alison and I would welcome him. Before, I wanted only to be with him, and we were each other's best friend. I'm sure my need to be with Alison will pass (it had better; she'd be miserable if it didn't), but we're still so close I don't want this time to be wasted. Soon enough she'll grow emotionally resistant again, as she should, but now she's still like a person turned inside out, still open to talking about feelings and caring and love and hurt. I'm so fiercely, intensely, enormously proud of her achievement. I want her to know how much I love her.

Thursday, November 7, 3:15 P.M.

Alison had another fitting for the new prosthesis today. I took the day off and drove her to Kessler. She had two drivers during the last weeks of therapy, both elderly, retired men. One, in particular, cared very much about her, but she didn't respond to his gentle concern, wanting to prove her independence to everyone, not just to me.

Alison's big day has come. We had her student driver's license validated this morning. Then, once we left the Turnpike coming back from Kessler, she drove home on back streets through fast-moving traffic. Both panic and pride were her passengers, but she's responsive to my direction and she'll learn well. I'll enjoy teaching her, as I enjoyed the lessons with the boys. Besides, we can talk in the car.

Friday, November 8, 8:00 P.M.

The breast biopsy involved a one-day trip in and out of the hospital. The tumor was benign, though the days leading up to this have been difficult, despite my best intentions, not only because of the normal terror of cancer that any woman facing a biopsy experiences, but because such a diagnosis would have forced me to confront the possibility of leaving Alison before she's ready. I can't conceive of dying until Alison is no longer vulnerable, until I'm certain that her strength is not fragile, her courage is not bravado, her wit is not a shield. I think that moment is quickly approaching; nevertheless, I don't intend to die.

Being in Englewood Hospital this morning brought back memories of the emergency room, Alison's ashen face, her shocked eyes, the swinging double doors through which I walked to hear, "She's going to lose her leg," and then out, to ride in the ambulance. And I thought of Alison's having to go through another operation, this time elective surgery. She must have the rod removed from the femur in any case, in a year or so, but she must also consider elective surgery to have the stump revised, shortened, so that she can wear a more cosmetic and sophisticated prosthesis. But whether such a prosthesis would be worth the apprehension, the pain, and the renewed dependence on me for a while only she can decide.

Monday, November 18, 8:00 P.M.

Snow, sleet, and pelting rain soaked the players, band members, and spectators at Saturday's football game in Tenafly. But Alison was there. "If I were playing with the marching band," she reasoned, "I'd have to be out there anyway." And so, feeling herself a member of the band, and of everything else, she huddled with the others in the bleachers. I worried about what would happen to the prosthesis—foam rubber over steel—if it became soaked. I had visions of her needing a can of oil like the *Wizard of Oz*'s Tin Man, or of her prosthesis becoming waterlogged and weighing twenty pounds. None of this happened; Alison, as always, took care of herself and kept the leg dry with a friend's blanket.

Sunday was another day of being part of "the gang." The temple youth group held a scavenger hunt in a shopping mall. A lot of running around in an attempt to win; hardly an activity for Alison. But she went along, helped the group's director get organized, cheered along the participants, rode on an escalator for the first time since the accident, and as she always does, did what she was able to do, without thinking, or at least appearing to, of what she was unable to do. "It wasn't getting me anywhere, being depressed," she told a girl who didn't know about and hadn't guessed the extent of Alison's injuries. Alison is happy when that happens, when someone thinks she merely hurt her leg.

Wednesday, November 20, 6:45 P.M.

Alison spent the afternoon at Kessler, for the second fitting of the new leg. When she got home she said that it didn't look very different from the leg she has now and that she's not ever planning to wear a skirt. She had high hopes for the way the new leg would look. But she'll have a suction socket, which means that she'll no longer need the heavy leather belt that snakes up one hip, wraps around her waist, and then snakes down the other hip to hold the prosthesis on.

Because the stump is the length it is, she'll still have what is called an extension on the knee, making her left thigh appear longer than her right when she sits but making it easier for her to walk. She no longer goes to Kessler at all, not even for swimming, and now the prosthetist thinks she won't need the sessions of physical therapy he had thought she'd require after she got the new leg.

Friday, November 22, 9:45 P.M.

I've seen so often a family's breakup after a tragedy— an illness or death, especially that of a child. I knew Charly's and my relationship was too steady for that to happen anymore, but I've missed the easy friendship we had and the way we could communicate without a word before the accident. It's coming back slowly. This evening he read the beginning of this journal, and his eyes filled. He hasn't cried since the first days after the accident.

It's only a few days until we will have passed four months. I've become accustomed to watching Alison walk, and I find her gait appealing: the thrust of her left hip, to activate the knee, the follow-through of the prosthesis; the deliberate pace differentiates her, just as her attitude does.

She's returned to the mainstream to such a degree that people are treating her as normally as she wants to be treated, and it's a measure of her capability that she can accept this more bruising way of life. The chemistry teacher who told Charly and me on Open School Night that he was in love with our daughter because he admired her so gave her a C+—her first ever—on her report card. She missed a B by two-tenths of a point, but it's a small disappointment in a life she's filling with satisfactions. And, when I pointed out to Dom Albanese that the parking spot designated for the handicapped outside the school would force Alison to walk across snow and wet grass to reach the crosswalk, he offered to give up his own more accessible space in the parking lot for her. But no longer do people think ahead for her, nor does she need it.

Though the C+ rankles her, she's earned A's and B's in her other subjects. Had she gotten C's and D's, I would have found that acceptable and predictable. She was able to overcome the disadvantages of home tutoring and missing three weeks of school, and to concentrate when so much else must have been on her mind.

But nothing is easy. Soon the school's ski club will begin its Friday evening ski trips, the ones Alison had participated in for four years. She may not even be allowed to try skiing yet. The last x ray, according to Dr. Jain, still showed signs of the pelvis and hip fractures. Until they're fully healed, the doctor doesn't want Alison to add further activity.

Alison has tried out for the school play, but she doesn't think she will get one of the big leads because they're dancing and singing parts.

The school music concert is a month from now. The chorus members will enter the auditorium from the back of the room, Alison tells me, and then fall into place on the risers in front of the stage. They can't walk at Alison's slower pace, so she'll have to meet them from a front seat and accompany them to the stage.

She doesn't bemoan. She doesn't cry. I'm still, four months later, waiting for something terrible to happen to her emotional stability, maybe because of the dire warnings of the Bellevue psychiatrists and the Kessler psychologist. But apparently the strength is real and the acceptance complete. Next Tuesday she returns to the psychologist here, who had faith in Alison's ability to cope without first plunging into a grief-stricken depression. Alison hasn't seen the psychologist for a month; she says this will be the last visit, and the psychologist agrees. It's evident that Alison gets up each day ready to try new challenges, ready to demonstrate new strengths.

Saturday, November 30, 11:00 P.M.

Jonathan was home for Thanksgiving, and this evening we all went to a Japanese restaurant both to celebrate being together and to celebrate, late, Charly's birthday six days ago. As we walked in, Alison lost her balance and fell, slowly, as she has done now and then. Immediately, Peter "fell" too, causing her to laugh and to overcome her embarrassment. She knows she has support, zany or otherwise.

Eleven

"...AND LEARN
TO FLY AGAIN"

Thursday, December 5, 10:30 P.M.

She wore her sleek, ankle-length black "concert" skirt and the silky white blouse I bought yesterday to bolster her confidence. She sang with the chorus as she's always sung, on the bottom riser, and I could hear her voice, though Charly tells me it's not possible to hear my children's voices separately from the others. I do.

Alison didn't stride in singing from the rear of the auditorium with the other choir members. She waited for them at the front row of seats and, in what has now become her singular gait, led them to their assigned places. In the darkened auditorium, few people saw the interchange. We watched her sing, proud that this radiant girl, our daughter, was where she was.

The concert band followed the chorus. The singers were expected to climb the risers to the stage to join the other musicians already assembled. With a hand on each of two people's shoulders, Alison negotiated the last high step up so that she could play her saxophone. If there were people in Cresskill who had worried about her, they could see her progress in that one action. Bravo, Cresskill. Brava, Alison.

Friday, December 6, 7:15 P.M.

Alison has her new prosthesis. It was painful the first few hours, and it's not the perfect leg she envisioned, but she's happy because it does resemble more closely the configuration of her own leg. She tells me she'll try wearing skirts now, something she hadn't contemplated before. "And," she says, "I might try swimming in the summer without a special prosthesis."

Saturday, December 7, 8:00 P.M.

Sean has asked Alison to go out with him, on a non-steady basis. He's apparently broken off his relationship with Erica, yet I can see, and I'm afraid Alison can't, that he still wants only to be with Erica. Gentle and kind soul that he is, I think he's reacting to Alison's recently having told him that she's loved him since last July. She said July 15; I didn't ask how she could so exactly know the date. He won't hurt Alison, I know, but I fear that his heart is with Erica and that Alison's heart could be broken.

Monday, December 9, 6:00 P.M.

Alison is rarely home after school anymore; she's rehearsing for the school play in March. Despite her earlier doubts, she's gotten one of the leading roles, fifteen-year-old Kim in *Bye, Bye Birdie*. She won't be able to dance in a role that calls for dancing, and her exits and entrances will have to be carefully staged, but she can sing in a role that calls for singing. The drama teacher kept his promise: he's willing to put in the extra effort to help Alison create Kim.

Tuesday, December 10, 7:00 A.M.

Yesterday was Jonathan's thirtieth birthday. Today is my fifty-second.

Thursday, December 19, 6:00 P.M.

Alison received a Christmas card from Dr. Livingston in answer to one we sent him and in which I related Alison's achievements and our gratitude for his part in them. He wrote that he is moving to another hospital, in the Midwest, next summer, but he gave us no forwarding address. We will likely lose touch with him after he leaves Bellevue. I hope someday he will meet Alison again.

Saturday, December 21, 4:00 P.M.

I rarely write anymore. I, too, am approaching a normal life. Partly it's because I'm busy, but mostly it's because I'm not as depressed anymore. Alison has resumed her school activities—play, chorus, concert band, yearbook, weekend parties, and friends, friends, friends. She's never discouraged, never moody. The rare times she's angry it's more than likely to be because her face has broken out before a date, because she's tired or hungry, or because she's got to memorize fifty chemistry symbols by Thursday or read three hundred pages for English by Monday.

Monday, December 30, 7:45 P.M.

"And learn to fly again . . ." Alison did, on snow, feeling again the exhilaration of speed of motion. She skied.

She was the one who drove early this morning to Vernon Valley, a feat in itself, an hour-long trip in rush-hour traffic on Route 80. We found the parking space for the handicapped directly in front of the entrance, forecasting a good day and officials sensitive to the needs of the disabled. I couldn't have known how much.

Once in the parking spot, however, and with no prosthesis along because she knew she'd have to ski with one leg only and in any case wouldn't be able to walk in snow with the prosthesis, Alison panicked. "No," she cried. "I can't get out of this car. I want to go home. I can't walk with my crutches all the way to the ski school up there. I don't want all those people to see me with one leg. I'm afraid. It's not worth it. I don't want to do it. I can't. Let's go home."

I got out of the car intending to find someone from the ski school who might help. The director pointed out a young instructor, Rick, walking toward the school hut. When I told Rick our dilemma, he spun around, followed me to the car and patiently convinced Alison to come out. He helped her cross the snow on her crutches, his hand always at her back. She was willing to try, for Rick.

For the rest of the morning they stayed on the beginner's slope, a hill she had left behind eight years earlier. Finally, she was able to negotiate the rope tow, an achievement even for someone with two skis and two legs. When she came inside at noon, she was exhausted and disheartened, having seemingly relearned not much more than how to stand on one ski and how to pick herself up after falling.

After she'd had lunch, Rick took her out again, for more than two hours. When she returned, her cheeks were flushed not only from the wind and the brilliant sunshine, but from exultation as well. She had ridden up on the chairlift and skied downhill with speed, and in control. All the way home she relived her joy, saying without words: I can do anything I want to do.

The entire day with Rick, the use of the special ski poles, which attach to the forearms like crutches and are equipped with little skis on the bottom of each, the use of the tow and the lift, surely that amounted to at least $100 worth of services from Vernon Valley. All of it cost just $10. "It's our contribution to the disabled," the director said. They contributed to Alison's soaring flight, psychological and physical, five months after she thought she would never fly again.

Wednesday, January 8, 1986, 9:00 P.M.

Sean took Alison skiing again today. She skied with Rick in the morning, until she was sure of her ability on the chair lift. The operators stopped the lift each time so that she could get off more easily at the top of the hill. Vernon Valley has perfected its contribution to the disabled.

Tuesday, January 14, 8:00 P.M.

I'm planning a surprise party for Alison's seventeenth birthday on January 31—fifty kids and ten adults, including three of her teachers and Jenni's and Linda's parents. Planning it is exciting; anticipating it is even more so. I'd love to share it with Alison; instead I confer with Linda and Jenni. Jenni, especially, is enjoying our clandestine discussions and her involvement in the preparations.

Alison's thoughts are only of the promised car. She has no idea that it's been in a neighbor's garage for more than four weeks, ever since it was delivered earlier than we had anticipated. We wanted it to be a birthday present and so quickly had to find a way to hide this huge gift. The generous neighbor is a woman who lives around the corner and is willing to give up her garage space because "we want to be part of Alison's birthday surprise." There are few people around who aren't involved with Alison in one way or another.

Wednesday, January 15, 8:15 P.M.

The newspaper published a follow-up story on Alison today. The earlier one, in September, had stressed her courage but also her pain and her loss. This one described her triumphs since then and was written so well that I've sent it to everyone who had any part in Alison's recovery: to Bellevue (Dr. Livingston and my one-time nemesis, the head nurse), to Kessler, to the transportation company. The article described Alison's ebullience, her full schedule, and her role in the school play as that of an upbeat student playing an upbeat part.

What the article didn't tell, and couldn't, and what I'm discovering as I reread my earlier notes, is the metamorphosis from desolation at Bellevue, to hope at Kessler, to self-confidence now. It has seemed like a slow evolution, yet it's been only five and a half months.

Sunday, January 19, 6:00 P.M.

Just as she did last year, Alison sang in concert with the Bergen County Chorus this afternoon, a position for which she had to audition last fall. Nothing had changed since we last saw her with the group; there in front of us was the same enchanting girl who lives in our house. Oh, yes, her voice has matured, and, yes, under the knee-length black skirt her left leg looks different, more artificial, than it did last year, and, yes, she walks with a limp. Except for the parents of other Cresskill students, few people in the audience could have known what it meant for Alison to be wearing a short skirt. Her father and her grandmothers and I knew.

Friday, January 24, 5:30 P.M.

We had an appointment with an orthopedist to discuss the removal of the rod in Alison's thigh and the possibility of revising the stump to enable use of a better prosthesis. The rod's removal is a minor operation requiring a day or so in the hospital and a few days at home. Revision would mean a longer hospital stay, considerably more pain, a new prosthesis, and the therapy needed to learn to use it. With or without the revision, Alison will have to be on crutches for six weeks. It would take that long for the stump to heal, and it would take that long for the femur to heal where the rod had been. But, as Alison walked away from him, the doctor observed her and mused, "Are you sure you want the revision? You're doing so well right now." That's all it took. No, she doesn't want the stump revised. She wants nothing changed and is satisfied with the way she walks, the way the prosthesis looks and performs, and with her life as it is. She was waiting for someone to say those words, but no one has wanted to influence her.

Just a week from today Alison will be seventeen, eligible for her driving test and to drive alone. She's getting nervous, hearing stories from her friends who have already passed—or failed—the test. I'm nervous too. I don't want her to fail; she wants so much to drive her car, she asks about it each day.

"Hasn't it come in yet? What if it doesn't get delivered before my birthday?"

"No, Alison, we haven't heard anything," I lie. "We'll have to call and find out what's happening."

Friday, January 31, 12:15 P.M.

It was still dark at seven this morning when Charly walked the half block to get the little red car and bring it into our driveway. It was still dark when he came into Alison's room to tell her to look out the window. "I'm late, Dad. I've got to get dressed for my eight o'clock driver's test," she grumbled.

"Go ahead, look outside. It's snowing." He tried again.

"Ohmygod," she shrieked. Had it not been for the silvery balloons Charly had tied to the aerial she might not have seen the car in the darkness, but their glimmer was enough to alert her to the shape beneath. Her car was here!

We arrived early for the driving test, early enough for her to panic as motor vehicle officials arrived and entered the building. We sat in the car, second in line. "See that old woman with the gray hair? That's the one they told me fails everyone. That's the one I'm going to get. I know it. Ohmygod." Moments later another "old" woman with gray hair arrived. And another. Each time the litany was repeated. Finally, a benign-looking man in an official brown uniform approached. I got out and found the best vantage point from which to try to observe, and he climbed in beside Alison. They drove straight ahead; she stopped cautiously at the stop sign that comes up immediately and then rounded a curve out of sight. My stomach was going around a curve too. It's only a driving test, I reasoned, she can take it again in a few weeks, but I knew she didn't feel that way. As she drove back from the course she looked tense until the inspector turned to her and said something. Then her smile and her shining eyes told me she had passed.

We went home; she slid into the driver's seat of her

own car, and drove—flew—off to school. So began her seventeenth birthday.

Saturday, February 1, 11:30 P.M.

The dining room was festooned in red and white crepe paper, balloons, streamers. The playroom downstairs was decorated in yellow and orange. The lights were out, the people were hushed. The garage door opened, the car pulled in. The kitchen door opened; Jenni and Linda walked in. Alison walked in, and then began a long story to Charly, who had been sitting alone in the kitchen as a "red herring," about the adventures the three of them had had at their dinner out. The telling was interminable. Finally, I stepped out of the darkness and directed her toward the dining room. Lights blazed. "Surprise!" "Ohmygod!"

There were youngsters everywhere. So many. But each one had had some part in Alison's recovery. Many had visited her in Bellevue. They had all supported her, then and in the time that followed. They were all her friends.

When Alison was called downstairs to meet the "gorilla," no one had any idea what the gorilla would do. When the furry creature turned out to be a male stripper—a secret gift from five of her friends—who wanted Alison's help in removing his clothes, Alison had the grace to blush, at least in front of her mother and father and social studies teacher. When the stripper was down to a two-inch-square black cloth and two strings interfering with total nudity, Alison's rite of passage was complete.

Alison's birthday cake, which I'd envisioned for weeks and had drawn out for the bakery, showed a bird in flight against a blue sky. Beneath were written the words to "Broken Wings"—"Take these broken wings/And learn to fly again/Learn to live so free."

There was one more symbol commemorating this birthday. When Alison was born I began the story of Alison's life with a charm bracelet, each year's charm representing a highlight of the twelve months before. Over time we've added a cat and a dog, a piano and a ballerina, a dollhouse and a telephone, a star of David and an Eiffel tower. Now a bird, its half-inch wingspread not nearly equaling what it represents, has taken its place on Alison's bracelet.

Sunday, February 8, 8:00 P.M.

Alison skied with a group organized by the physical therapists at Kessler. She hasn't participated before in any of Kessler's recreational offerings for amputees. Remembering her hesitation about appearing with others in wheelchairs at the Bruce Springsteen concert shortly after she arrived at Kessler, I wasn't sure what her reaction to today's trip would be. But I should have known. She returned happy, full of enthusiasm for the new friends she'd made, the experiences they'd shared, and the amputee stories they'd related.

Friday, February 14, 6:00 P.M.

The attitude Alison has adopted—I'll do what I can and not worry about what I can't—has prompted us to encourage her to take voice lessons. Her first was today. She's excited about the play, just three weeks from now, but she's tense because the newspaper article in January has brought us dozens of requests for tickets from many of our friends who had read the article about her.

Alison said she'd be home late from school, that she was going to watch her friends jump rope to raise money for the Heart Fund.

"It's going to be depressing, watching them and not being able to do anything," she said.

"Then why are you going?"

"I still want to be a part of what's going on. It's better than staying home."

That evening, in a casual mention that I caught as Alison passed by me, she said, "I tried jump roping. I did it, for several minutes, on one foot."

Saturday, February 15, 3:00 P.M.

The relationship with Sean is over. As I'd suspected, his heart was with Erica, though that hasn't diminished his love for Alison. She's hurt, because she didn't really know about his continuing desire for Erica. Nor did she know, though I suspected, that more often than not he went from our house directly to Erica's. But Alison knows he will always be a friend. I think she knows, too, that her dating Sean was a mistake; the friendship is not.

But the kittens are ours. Peter wants us to keep them. I think he planned it that way, as his gift to us.

Friday, March 7, 11:00 P.M.

We had not intended to offer tickets to tonight's performance, the first of the weekend. I wanted the first evening alone with Charly in the dark auditorium, so that if I cried I would cry alone. But one couple from out of town couldn't attend any other performance. Their pride in Alison nearly matched ours, and their tears were as quick as mine were. We were glad they were there to appreciate Alison's triumph with us as we waited for her to disengage herself from the other actors to greet us after the play's conclusion. But we weren't the only ones cheering Alison this evening. Besides the Cresskill people in the audience, who knew and remembered, two elderly men approached me as we waited for her.

"Mrs. Lehmann?" one said, extending his hand. Seeing my lack of recognition, he continued. "You don't remember us. We were Alison's drivers from the transportation company. We saw the article you sent to the office and we wanted to make the trip to see her. She was wonderful, beautiful. We are so proud of her."

Saturday, March 9, 11:30 P.M.

If last night was the time to contemplate, to appreciate, tonight was the time to rejoice. We invited everyone who attended tonight's performance to have dinner with us beforehand. It was a party of Alison's admirers, with people coming from Missouri (Jonathan), Washington, D.C. (Peter), Long Island (Nancy,

Alison's cousin, and her husband), Connecticut (Eric, my former colleague), northwest New Jersey (Nora Palmieri—who walks well now—and her husband), southern New Jersey (Alison's therapist from Kessler), and from every town around (our temple friends). There were no tears tonight. There was pride, multiplied by the fifty people who surrounded us in the auditorium. Alison was charming, both singing and speaking, as Kim. Her entrances and exits were directed with sensitivity. When the others danced, a time of regret for me last night, she stood aside, still in character, while I watched the extraordinary character that Alison has become.

Tomorrow afternoon there's one more performance, the one the grandmothers will attend, together with Alison's friends from other schools and still more friends of ours. Alison has reached the peak of self-confidence and ebullience this weekend.

Wednesday, March 20, 6:00 P.M.

Alison has found a person to whom she can talk at any time, and about anything. Irene Shubsda, her guidance counselor, discusses with her far more than her senior-year courses or visits to college campuses. She talks with her, but more important, she listens, and she hears.

Since Alison's return to school, Irene, who had not seen her in the hospital or at home, confessed to me that she didn't know how to approach her, to talk to her. "Just talk to her—about the accident, about what's happened—she'll respond," I suggested. The response has been two-way. Irene has become another important person in Alison's life.

Saturday, March 29, 1:00 P.M.

For two weeks there's been a new love in Alison's life. Jon Rose, a big, bulky ice hockey player with kind blue eyes and straw-colored hair that won't lie flat, looks more as if he could melt the heart of a girl teddy bear than that of a teenage girl. But he's melted Alison's as no one has before. She told me he said, "I don't care what you have or what you don't have. I love you just the way you are." The words I wanted a man to say to her. It may be too soon and it may be impermanent, but now she's heard those words and knows they can be said.

Wednesday, April 2, 8:30 A.M.

Alison, talking about Jon Rose, about her life as it is now, about her achievements, said to me this morning, "This has been the best year."

Monday, April 7, 5:00 P.M.

Alison and I visited a doctor in New York who specializes in liver diseases. A blood test performed by her gynecologist a few weeks ago revealed that one of the twelve units of blood she received on July 25 had a hepatitis virus in it. It's a strain called non-A, non-B type, the doctor said, transmissible only through blood transfusions. It hasn't manifested itself in any way. She's missed no school this year because of illness. We would not have known of this if I hadn't asked for her blood to be tested because she has been having irregular menstrual periods. There is a possibility of future complications, but the doctor believes a cure will be found even if they do occur because of all the testing being done for AIDS, which he says may have an impact on help for this type hepatitis as well. We'll have to believe that and believe also that Alison's good health and her enthusiasm for life will preclude future problems.

Saturday, April 26, 9:00 P.M.

In a year and a half Alison will enter college. Because the operation for removal of the rod looms next fall, we've begun looking at colleges now, so far all in Pennsylvania. The three of us visited two Thursday, two yesterday, and one, the one she favors, today. It's only two hours away, the campus is flat and compact— both important features for her—and she liked the atmosphere and the people. I wish I could make it easy for her and do the admitting. She'll have to apply and then wait. I'd like her not to be disappointed, but I know she can handle disappointment.

It was painful for her to tour the campuses, especially because she needs a new socket in the prosthesis. It's due to be fitted next week, and her capacity for walking these past days was even more limited than usual. In every case, though, the admitting office arranged for a private tour for us so that she wouldn't have to keep up the pace and distance of the group tours.

Tuesday, May 6, 10:00 P.M.

It is an honor to be inducted into the National Honor Society in the junior year of high school. Alison was inducted tonight.

Thursday, May 8, 11:00 P.M.

There was another concert in the high school tonight, the spring concert. This time Alison cared only that Jon Rose was in the audience. She is always happy.

She had been told already, and it was announced tonight, that her audition for the All State Chorus had been successful. She'll be singing with other New Jersey choristers next January.

Friday, May 30, 7:30 P.M.

For five minutes Alison's story was told on CBS's local news this evening in a segment entitled "Positively Yours." Last month when I first saw the segment, which features people with a positive outlook, I wrote two paragraphs to the news anchor suggesting Alison as a subject. When I didn't hear further, I forgot about it, thinking they probably were looking for groups of people or for different types of people. On Monday, the show's producer, apologizing for "bothering" me on a holiday—Memorial Day—called to ask if Alison would be available for filming on Wednesday and whether she would mind being interviewed. Alison knew nothing of the letter, but outwardly calm, she agreed, to much razzing from her friends at Tammy Brook, where she took the call.

On Wednesday, the TV team followed her for four hours, through the school and to Tammy Brook. On Friday we watched, together with hundreds of thousands of other New York area viewers, the girl the anchorman called "a courageous girl from Cresskill, New Jersey." Alison was shown walking around the school grounds with CBS's anchorwoman, Michelle Marsh, driving off in her red car, and generously plying mustard on a hot dog at the snack bar at Tammy Brook, all the time answering Ms. Marsh's questions.

"Were you angry?" Ms. Marsh asked.

"Yes, because I knew nothing was going to happen to the driver. He damaged my whole life."

Charly summarized it. "As I told my wife," he said, "I don't think you'll have to console her. She's the one who'll give you courage."

And she has.

Tuesday, June 4, 7:00 A.M.

Alison hasn't yet seen the TV interview. She's been away. Every four years the marching band goes on a six-day trip to Disney World, timed so that each band member gets to Florida once while in high school. This was the year, and Alison was with them. Maybe it wasn't just the way she's anticipated it since she was a freshman, but she was no less excited than had she participated in the concert the band presents at the theme park. And the trip occasioned two big break-throughs in Alison's recovery. After twenty-four hours on a bus, the youngsters were hot and tired. Upon their arrival they found relief in the motel pool. Alison was right in there with them, all one hundred and fifty of them. The swimming barrier was broken.

When she arrived at the park early the next morning, Alison faced fifteen hours of racing from exhibit to exhibit with exuberant, hardy youngsters. She knew she couldn't keep up with them for even a fraction of the time. For the first time, recognizing her limitations, she consented to using a wheelchair. The day was a success: she was comfortable and happy, and the other kids didn't have to leave her behind. Another barrier was broken, in such a way that Alison knew her decision wasn't a step backward, wasn't abandonment of her resolve, but was a realistic assessment of her situation. The teachers who were along were so touched by her courageous decision and her cheerful spirit that they bought her a souvenir stuffed animal. "Figment" has joined the gang in her room.

Tuesday, June 10, 6:00 P.M.

"I can't take any more disappointments. Why did this have to happen just when everything was so great?" she wailed. Jon Rose is leaving; he'll spend his senior year at a high school in Iowa. He's been chosen to be a member of a national junior ice hockey team, but to take advantage of the opportunity he must leave Cresskill for Iowa, where the team is situated. She's crushed at the thought of spending the next school year without this friend who's been so good for her, but at the same time she's proud of what he's accomplished—if only it could have been accomplished here.

Friday, June 20, 2:30 P.M.

Alison spent the past five days at Rutgers College as her school's representative to the state Woman's Club Citizenship Week. As she's been doing for the past month, she wore shorts down to the college. The other girls must have wondered what happened to this pretty, vivacious girl with the artificial leg, but they didn't ask. The first speaker, she said, addressed the rights of victims of crime. He himself had been such a victim and had been blinded in one eye after a mugging. He asked his young audience whether any of them had had a similar experience. In front of three hundred girls, all strangers, Alison rose to tell her story. As she had in Cresskill, she sensed immediately the other girls' warmth and support and empathy. By Alison's reaching out to the others, putting them at ease as she's been doing since the first days at Bellevue, she made it easy for them to respond to her.

Later in the week she joined two others girls to sing a trio during the evening entertainment, though she hadn't intended to sing other than with the choir they would pull together for the week. By last night the other girls had persuaded Alison to sing a solo on Thursday evening. When she finished singing "What I Did for Love" she found herself receiving a standing ovation.

Two more barriers tumbled this week. Alison knows now that she can move beyond Cresskill and still find people who will care about her, and she knows that she will be able to function well in a college dormitory situation.

Sunday, June 22, 5:00 P.M.

Much as I like to walk with Charly when we're away from home, I like the strolls we take in our own neighborhood more. Few of the houses that once looked alike still resemble each other. Over three decades people have rebuilt their homes, just as we have, and we follow the progress of renovation along our routes. We stop to talk with the people we see, whose first question is always: "How is Alison?"

It's easier for us to walk in Cresskill because after that question we can go on to other topics. No further explanations are needed and no past experiences must be described. We talk about our jobs, the weather, the grass, the neighbors, just as they do. We renovated our house so as to stay in Cresskill, on the street where we've raised all of our children. Cresskill has been a town where people don't compete with each other, except on the football field. The town is not idyllic; people have problems here just as they do everywhere else. But most people care about their families and their homes, and the sense of peace Charly and I feel here is a reflection of that. The support the town has given Alison has been like the wound on a tree when it closes in on itself, affording protection.

Charly and I have found peace also with each other. He's become again the same irascible but gentle, kind, and loving person he's always been. He no longer has to express his pain and loss through senseless anger. Now he explodes momentarily, Alison and I ignore him, and it's all over in a minute. We can live with that. We've been doing it for a long time. I wouldn't want anything in my life with him to change.

Thursday, July 24, 10:30 P.M.

It was a Thursday, a year ago, when I began writing Alison's story. I had no way of knowing what I would be writing now. I knew that her leg could not be replaced, but I didn't know that her courage could unfold as it has.

In the month since I've last written, school ended and Alison got the report card she wanted: all A's and B-plusses—even in chemistry. She's back at work at Tammy Brook, where she's treated like everyone else. I believe that's as it should be.

She faced another fear: the ocean. Jonathan and Peter went to the beach with us when they were here for Peter's twenty-third birthday, over July Fourth weekend. Alison slipped off the prosthesis while she sat on the blanket and attracted no attention, but when the boys got ready to go into the water she knew she had to get up on her crutches and walk to the water. She balked. We persuaded. She went. At the water's edge I took the crutches from her and, holding on to each of her brothers' shoulders and with their arms at her waist, she hopped into the sea. The last barrier crashed along with the waves.

She knows not all days will be filled with triumphs and achievements. Sad events will always happen. Yesterday we found Ophelia, our shy little kitten, dead in a neighbor's yard. Despite Alison's sorrow, compounded by her dread of the anniversary of the accident, she's accepting this, too.

In a month she'll go to Hawaii. The idea of a special swim leg has long been forgotten. She plans to swim and sightsee and snorkel and paraglide.

Friday, July 25, 10:00 A.M.

A story related to me: several of the high school's teachers were sitting in their lounge discussing the feasibility of the students' wearing shorts to classes.

"Alison Lehmann is wearing shorts today," one teacher said.

"Really? I hadn't noticed," said another.

ABOUT THE MAKING OF THIS BOOK

The text of *All I Could Do Was Love You* was set in Baskerville by ComCom, a division of Haddon Craftsmen, Inc. of Allentown, Pennsylvania. The book was printed by the Maple-Vail Book Manufacturing Group of Binghamton, New York. The typography and binding were designed by Tom Suzuki of Falls Church, Virginia.